The Ridouts of Sherborne
Dorset family history

Karen Francis

Karen Francis
2014

Copyright © 2014 by Karen Francis

All rights reserved. This book or any portion thereof may not be reproduced or used in any manner whatsoever without the express written permission of the publisher except for the use of brief quotations in a book review or scholarly journal.

First Printing: 2014

ISBN: 978-1-326-10885-4

Published by the author
3 Durlston Close, Cardiff CF14 2LY

www.the-ridouts.com

Contents

Table of Figures vi
Acknowledgements ix
Introduction 1
1. John Ridout (1785-1855): my x3 great grandfather 3
2. Charles and Samuel Ridout: my x3 great uncles 6
3. Ridouts, Rideouts and a tangled web of yDNA 9
4. William Ridowte of Hyle (1554ª-1621) 13
5. Christopher Ridout of Henstridge (bp.1664): The Ridout Act 17
6. Christopher Ridout of Sherborne (bp.1669): The miller 20
7. Hyle Farm, Limekiln Farm and Ridout's Mill 27
8. Linking William of Hyle and Christopher Ridout 32
9. George Ridout (1701-1779): baker of West Mill 34
10. Exploding the myth: Huguenot Ridouts! 39
11. John Ridout of Sherborne to John Ridout of Bath 43
12. 'John Ridout IV' (c.1753-1827): man of mystery 46
13. Nethercombe Ridouts in Sherborne: is this my family? 49
14. London Ridouts: yellow shoes and blue murder! 54
15. Elizabeth Oliver & Alice Toogood 68
16. The Oliver family of Sherborne 72
17. The Ridouts of North Wootton 78
18. Richard of Folke & Richard of North Wootton 90
19. William Rydeowte of Chettle: a 16th century gentleman 98
20. Walter Rydowte of Folke (1564-1643): gentleman & rebel 109
21. An investigation of Ridout heraldry 123
22. Summary and Conclusions 144

Table of Figures

	page
1. 1851 census for John Ridout	3
2. St James's church, Bath	4
3. Sherborne Abbey	6
4. Slave cargo. Maryland Gazette, 1767	9
5. William Ridowte's will, 1620	13
6. 1930 map of Dorset, Maltkiln Hill	18
7. The Ridout Bill, 1696	19
8. John Ridout's will, 1678	20
9. Sherborne Abbey	21
10. Hyle Farm and West Mill, 1887	25
11. Christopher Ridout's signature, 1743	28
12. Ridout's Mill (West Mill), Sherborne	30
13. Ridout House, Annapolis, c. 1930	35
14. Sherborne Mercury, 1780; sale of Ridout's Mill	38
15. Thomas Ridout	39
16. Thomas Gibbs Ridout	40
17. Walter Ridout's bequest to Fontmell church, 1582	42
18. John Ridout's baptism, 1785	43
19. John and Susanna's marriage, 1781	44
20. Bristol Mercury banner	47
21. St Cuthbert's, Wells	50
22. Company of Cordwainers	54
23. The Great Synagogue, Duke's Place, ~1820	56
24. Tomb inscription	58
25. Dr John Gibbs Ridout attends the birth of Sarah	59
26. Freedom admission for Jeremiah Ridout, 1733	61
27. Rear of 21 & 22 Cloth Fair, c. 1904	62
28. Thomas Ridout shoes made between 1750 and 1770	64
29. Thomas Ridout's apprenticeship indenture, 1682	66
30. Christopher Oliver's will, 1687	73
31. Descendants of Christopher and Margaret Oliver	77
32. St Peter's church, North Wootton	79
33. Public notice, London Gazette 1805	84
34. Royal Fort, Bristol	85
35. Abbey Grange, Sherborne	87
36. 1930 map of Dorset, Lillington	91

37. St Lawrence's church, Folke	92
38. Richard Ridout's baptism in North Wootton, 1620	95
39. Wax seal of Sherborne School, 16thC	98
40. Plan of Sherborne School	100
41. Sir Nicholas Bacon	101
42. William Rydowte's accounts for Sherborne School	102
43. William Ridout's accounts for the Almshouse	103
44. St Mary's church, Chettle	105
45. Walter Rideout's accounts for Sherborne School	110
46. Walter's epitaph in Folke Church	113
47. Ridout arms from Chadwick	124
48. Roydon arms in trick	125
49. Marble bust of Joan St John	127
50. Family tree: Roydon of Battersea, Pyrford & Chertsey	128
51. Drawing of Stowe MSS 677 f23	131
52. Bookplate of Christopher Ridout	133
53. Armorial signet ring	134
54. Arms of Ridout	136
55. Trotting horse & savage's head crests on a wreath of the colours	137
56. Arms of Henry Wood Rideout	139
57. Arms of Richard Ridout	139
58. Arms of Arthur Kennedy Rideout	140

Image Credits:

Figs. 1, 5, 14, 17, 25: The National Archives, Kew, Surrey.
Figs. 2, 6, 7, 9, 10, 12, 13, 20, 21, 22, 27, 31, 34, 35, 36, 46, 47, 49, 51, 53 & 54: Author's own collection of old books, newspapers, photographs, postcards and maps, either purchased or donated.
Fig. 3: The Greater Abbeys of England (1908) Gasque, Francis & Aiden; published in New York by Dodd, Mead & Co.
Fig. 4: US Library of Congress. Maryland Gazette, 1 October 1767 (image 413).
Figs. 8, 11 & 30: Wiltshire & Swindon History Centre, Chippenham, Wiltshire
Fig. 15: Ten years of Upper Canada in peace and war, 1805-1815: being the Ridout letters (1890) Thomas Ridout; Matilda Ridout; published in Toronto by W. Briggs.
Fig. 16: Courtesy of Toronto Public Library.
Figs. 18, 19 & 38: Ancestry.co.uk website (www.ancestry.com).

Figs. 23, 32, 37, 41, 43 & 44: Wikimedia (www.commons.wikimedia.org).

Fig. 24: Memorials of the Old Meeting House and Burial Ground ed. Catherine Hutton Beale (1882); printed in Birmingham, England.

Figs. 26 & 29: Courtesy of London Metropolitan Archives, 40 Northampton Rd, London.

Fig. 28: Brooklyn Museum Costume Collection at The Metropolitan Museum of Art, Gift of the Brooklyn Museum, 2009; Gift of Charles Blaney, 1926 (2009. 300.1406a, b).

Fig. 33: Courtesy of London Gazette (www.london-gazette.co.uk).

Figs. 39, 42, 43 & 45: Courtesy of Sherborne School & Sherborne Almshouse via Dorset History Centre, Bridport Rd., Dorchester, Dorset.

Fig. 40: The Sherborne Register 1823-1900 (1900) H. H. House. 2nd ed. T. C. Rogerson, printed in Sherborne by F. Bennett.

Figs. 48 & 50: Three Royden Families (1924) Ernest Bland Royden; published in Edinburgh by R. & R. Clark Limited.

Figs. 52, 56 & 57: Courtesy of the Bookplate Society, London.

Fig. 55: Fairburn's Crests of the Leading Families in Great Britain and Ireland and Their Kindred in Other Lands (1911) James Fairburn; published in New York by Heraldic Publishing Company.

Fig. 58: Armorial Families: A Directory of Some Gentlemen of Coat-Armour, Showing which Arms in Use at the Moment are Borne by Legal Authority. 3rd edition (1899) Arthur Charles Fox-Davies; published in London by T.C. & E.C. Jack.

Acknowledgements

Family history would be a lonely pursuit if it were not for other like minded individuals with whom one shares ideas. I have been lucky enough to have had the help and support of numerous colleagues and Ridout family historians across the world, many of whom I have never met in person and probably never will. So… my grateful thanks to Barry Rideout, John Templeton, Carole Jamieson, Bill Archerd and a host of others.

Although many records can be found online these days, fortunately there is still much pleasure to be had from poring over old books and dusty papers in the local and national archives with which we are still blessed. Although I can't name any one person, I thank all of the very helpful staff and volunteers that I've met through the years at the National Archives at Kew, the Dorset History Centre in Dorchester and the Family History Centre, Museum, School and Almshouse at Sherborne.

Finally, my special thanks go to Angela for her encouragement and for her thorough editing of the finished article; also to my friends and family, who persuaded me that this was a worthwhile and achievable project (and who promised to buy a copy!).

Introduction

My Ridout family have lived in the city of Bath for over two hundred years and for most of my life it had never occurred to me that they might have lived anywhere else so it was quite a surprise when I found that our ancestral home was actually the lovely town of Sherborne in Dorset. In 2006, DNA testing hinted that this was where our Ridout roots were deepest and that my branch was somehow part of an old and well established tree. This book is the result of my research into the Sherborne branch of Ridouts. I have tried to source all my material as diligently as possible but I do not profess this to be a learned text; it is an amended version of an online blog [www.the-ridouts.com], hopefully now in a more durable format.

For many family historians, being able to trace an ancestral line back through the centuries is difficult, sometimes even impossible. Fortunately for me, Mr Arthur George Ridout (1852-1939), a grandson of Dr. John Gibbs Ridout (1757-1823), was as passionate about our family history as I am; armed with a pencil and notebook he visited Somerset House, the British Library and many other archives, some of which have since closed. Over many years Arthur, his wife Beaujolais and son Lionel recorded detailed information about various Ridout families and corresponded with distant relatives all over the world exchanging genealogical information. Arthur's many notebooks were later patiently transcribed, collated and digitised by the late Bill Ridout of Berkhamsted. Bill's transcription can be found in print form on the family history shelves of the Society of Genealogists in London [The Ridout Collection: Ridout, Arthur George 1998 Ref: FH/RID]. Although I have often consulted Arthur's research, I haven't always agreed with his interpretation of historical events or the family trees that he constructed. I have referred the reader throughout to the appropriate page of the 'Ridout book' for comparison purposes.

This is my understanding of my family's history and I fully accept and expect that I will have made mistakes; maybe they will corrected by someone else at some point in the future. I think that every piece of knowledge, added to the whole story, will hopefully add up one day to our best estimate of the truth.

Karen Francis

1. John Ridout (1785-1855): my x3 great grandfather

In the early days of my genealogical research, knowing my maternal grandfather's name and birth year, I was able to search back through online UK census records quite quickly and so it was in 1851 that I came 'face to face' with my x3 great grandfather John Ridout and was surprised to see that he was from Sherborne in Dorset (Fig. 1) when all the family that I had known were Bathonians.

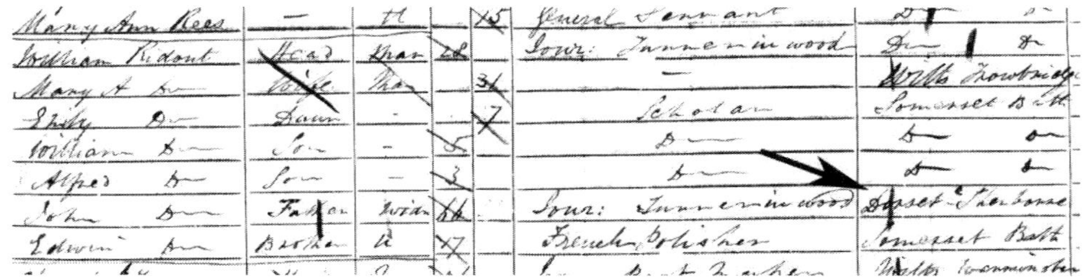

Mary Ann Rees	—	U	15	General Servant	Do
William Ridout	Head	Mar	28	Jour: Turner in wood	Do
Mary A Do	Wife	Mar	31	—	Wilts Trowbridge
Emily Do	Daur	-	7	Scholar	Somerset Bath
William Do	Son	-	5	Do	Do
Alfred Do	Son	-	3	Do	Do
John Do	Father	Widr	66	Jour: Turner in wood	Dorset Sherborne
Edwin Do	Brother	U	27	French Polisher	Somerset Bath

Figure 1: 1851 census for John Ridout

On a whim, I searched the internet for 'Ridout AND Sherborne' and came up with hits from America and Canada - people that were pioneers, bankers and politicians. This large Sherborne Ridout dynasty was well documented and there's a whole collection of papers about them at the Society of Genealogists, but my x3 grandfather was just a cabinet-maker; surely my little twig couldn't be connected to this mighty tree?

My x3 great grandfather was baptised in Sherborne Abbey, Sherborne in Dorset on the 12th February 1785 to John and Susanna Ridout. His three score years and ten spanned a very interesting period of history. Probably, as a youngster, John was told about the ongoing war with France but when Napoleon finally met his Waterloo, I wonder if the boy knew that a man named Sir George Ridout Bingham was in charge of guarding the defeated general on St Helena? Britain was still at war, this time in the Crimean peninsula, when John's life ended in 1855; he had outlived his parents, three siblings, two wives and nine out of thirteen of his children. I like to think of him as a sober, hard working and pious man but of course I'll never know if that's true.

Figure 2: St James's church, Bath

In 1807, slavery had been formally abolished in Great Britain and the Napoleonic Wars were in full swing; Admiral Lord Nelson had met his end at the battle of Trafalgar, William Pitt the Younger had expired, perhaps from an excess of fine port and 'Farmer' George III was still on the throne. According to a local Bath newspaper dated 6th May of that year, Jane Austen had, in her own view, 'escaped' the confines of the city to enjoy the breeziness of Clifton Downs in nearby Bristol. Lilac and apple blossom were the season's colours for fashionable young ladies, free smallpox inoculations were being administered at the City Dispensary and Dr Soloman was laying extravagant claims that his Cordial Balm of Gilead would cure most every ailment under the sun.

Earlier this same week, unreported by the local press, John Ridout, twenty-two year old cabinet-maker, married Sarah HODGES at St James' church, Southgate in Bath (Fig. 2).

Although there is no evidence to support it, I wondered if Sarah was John's apprentice master's daughter. If he had started a seven year cabinet maker's apprenticeship when he was fourteen he would have just finished serving his indentures by 1807. Sarah's father's name was William and there were several men named William Hodges in Bath directories of the time, including more than one cabinet maker. The relationship between John and the Hodges family is speculative, but what is clear is that at some point John left rural Dorset and headed for the still fashionable Somerset city where no doubt the market for fine furniture, although waning, exceeded that in Sherborne. The discovery of John Ridout's birth in Dorset started me on a ten year journey to find the family to which he, and of course I, belong. It was the beginning of my research into the history of the Ridouts of Sherborne.

2. Charles and Samuel Ridout: my x3 great uncles

My x3 great grandfather John Ridout did not grow up alone; the registers of Sherborne Abbey (Fig. 3) also record the following baptisms and burials:

- 19th July 1783: James, son of John & Susanna buried
- 25th December 1787: Charles, son of John & Susanna baptised
- 25th December 1790: Sarah, daughter of John & Susanna baptised
- 2nd December 1792: Ann, child of John & Susanna buried
- 29th June 1793: Alice, daughter of John & Susanna baptised
- 23rd January 1796: Samuel, son of John & Susanna baptised
- 16th February 1808: Alice, daughter of John & Susanna buried

Figure 3: Sherborne Abbey

For some reason the name Charles is unlucky for me, genealogically speaking; such men in my family seem either to die young or disappear without trace from the records. Unlike John, who I feel I have come to know well over the years, his brother Charles is a complete mystery. He may have stayed in Sherborne, at least until he married in the Abbey on 12th April 1815. His bride was Mary TOWERS, the daughter of William and Mary (née COTTELL); William Towers was the editor of the Sherborne Mercury. William and Mary's son William was a watchmaker in Wincanton who, the Bridgwater Advertiser published, died aged 44 at his mother's home in Sherborne on the 6th May 1833; in 1841 his sister Ann was a patient at the Forston Lunatic Asylum in Charminster and died shortly after this.

At some point in their marriage, Charles and Mary Ridout moved to Bath because, ten years apart, this is where both of them died. The couple worshipped at the Argyle Independent Chapel in Grove Street, Bathwick (Congregationalist) and were buried at Snow Hill by the chapel's most eminent divine, Reverend William Jay, who preached at Bath between 1790 and 1853. When Charles' wife Mary died, in August 1822, her address was recorded as 'Oak Street', a short road of terraced houses which still stands on the south side of the river. Although the couple were together seven years I couldn't find any infant baptisms in the church registers of Sherborne or Bath. At the time of his own death in March 1832, Charles' address was 'Orange Court', a small area behind the City Market, off Orange Grove. I was unable to find any evidence of Charles having paid rates in Bath but, given the number of rate books extant, this is still a work in progress. He is not recorded in the few existing early street or trade directories but these tended mainly to record the nobility, professional classes and clergy, rather than the general populace. When one has very little evidence one clutches at straws and so when I saw that 'Mr' Charles Ridout's death, "after a short illness", was reported in the local press, sitting amidst three 'Esquires', one 'Surgeon', one 'Lady' and four 'Reverends' I conferred an imaginary title of 'Gentleman' upon the poor fellow.

John Ridout's younger brother Samuel went to London at some point and married Elizabeth RADNOR, a lady from Diddlebury in Shropshire. Rather mysteriously, the couple called the banns but then didn't marry until two years later! Originally their wedding should have been within a very few days of 22nd December 1822, but it seems that they may not have turned up to the church on two of the three Sundays. Helpfully however, the pre-banns indicated that Samuel was lodging at 7 Portman Square and Elizabeth at 7 Little Ebury Street, both in what is now the London borough of Westminster. In 1824, the wedding finally took place at St Marylebone on 19th July. However, before he married, Samuel witnessed the marriage of John Arkill and Eliza Richards. In turn the newly married couple then witnessed Samuel and Elizabeth's marriage. Were these just strangers helping one another out or did the parties know one another? Samuel and Elizabeth had their first two children baptised at St Marylebone: William was born at Edgware Road on the 30th April 1825 (bp. 3rd August) and George was born at Seymour Place on the 28th February 1828 (bp. 7th June).

Although there have been UK censuses since 1801, most of them before 1841 are of little use to a family historian who wants names because they were conducted to collect statistical data such as the numbers of men, women and children or the different occupations in any one area. Fortunately though, Marylebone is one of the few districts in which the enumerator, for some reason, recorded names as well as numbers. In 1831, there was an entry: 'Ridout, Brown Street, Marylebone'. Not much, but exciting all the same. Samuel didn't make it to a trade directory until 1833 when Robson's London Directory listed 'Samuel Ridout, 22 Brown Street, Cheesemonger'. This came as a bit of a surprise because the children's baptisms and 1841 and 1851 censuses suggested that Samuel was a carpenter, joiner or builder. Why on earth was he listed as a cheesemonger? Was this a mistake or was this another man? In a bit of lateral thinking, I searched for information on John Arkill. The London Gazette of 14th November 1834 recorded the details of the Court for Insolvent Debtors, held at 9am on the 8th December at Portugal Street, off the Tottenham Court Road: 'John Arkill, late of No. 2, Tottenham-Street, Tottenham Court-Road, Middlesex, formerly a Cheesemonger, Pork-Butcher and French Polisher, and latterly a Dealer in Coals, Wood, Oysters, Butter, and Cheese'. So, I think it is no coincidence that John Arkill and Samuel Ridout had, at some point in their lives, been cheesemongers. I think they were friends when they witnessed each other's marriages and possibly even worked together for a while in the 1830s.

Samuel and his family moved to Dorking in Surrey where two more children were baptised together on the 5th July 1837 at the West Street Independent Chapel (Congregationalist) by the Reverend Richard Connebee; Alfred was born in Marylebone on the 10th April 1831 and Alice in St George's Westminster on the 26th December 1834. For some reason, Samuel and Elizabeth moved away from the established church and become non-conformists like both Samuel's brothers, John and Charles. In due course, the family moved back to London where perhaps their descendants may live still.

3. Ridouts, Rideouts and a tangled web of yDNA

In 2006, the late Bill Ridout invited me to meet him and his American friend Orlando in Dorset. I had heard of Orlando Ridout IV because in that year he made a public apology to Alex Haley, author of 'Roots: The Saga of an American Family'. Haley had claimed descendancy from a young warrior called Kunta Kinte, who'd been captured in 1767 from Julfureh (a village in the Gambia) and along with others was sold into slavery and shipped to Annapolis in Maryland aboard the Lord Ligonier. Orlando had apologised to Haley because the owner of the 'cargo' was Orlando's ancestor, John Ridout (Fig. 4).

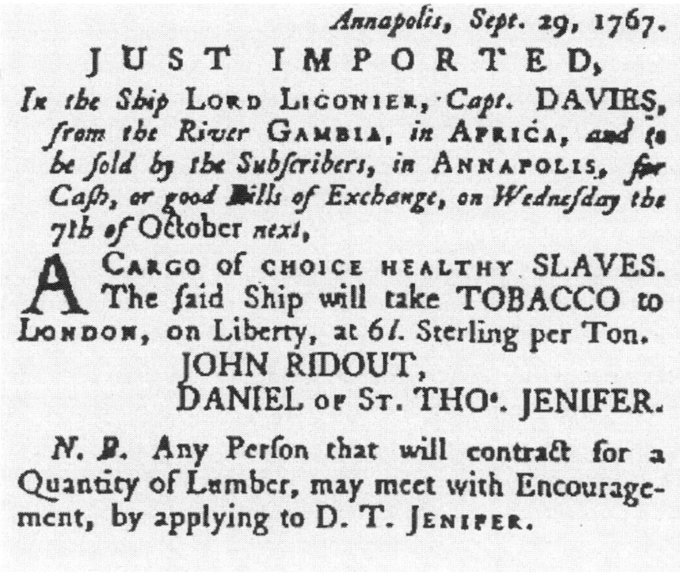
Annapolis, Sept. 29, 1767.

JUST IMPORTED,

In the Ship LORD LIGONIER, *Capt.* DAVIES, *from the River* GAMBIA, *in* AFRICA, *and to be ſold by the Subſcribers, in* ANNAPOLIS, *for Caſh, or good Bills of Exchange, on Wedneſday the 7th of* October *next,*

A CARGO of CHOICE HEALTHY SLAVES. The ſaid Ship will take TOBACCO to LONDON, on Liberty, at 6*l.* Sterling per Ton.

JOHN RIDOUT,
DANIEL OF ST. THO^{s}. JENIFER.

N. B. Any Perſon that will contract for a Quantity of Lumber, may meet with Encouragement, by applying to D. T. JENIFER.

Figure 4: Slave cargo. Maryland Gazette, 1767

Orlando Ridout IV is a very pleasant gentleman – he, Bill and I happily toured Dorset villages for the day, sharing a lunch and some genealogical chatter at a pub in Henstridge. Before we parted company, Orlando gave me a yDNA kit and asked me if I could find a male family member to send off a sample of saliva. He wanted to see how several Dorset Ridouts were related to him and to each other. I did as he asked and, a few weeks later, the results came back. Much to my surprise, my cousin's yDNA matched exactly to Orlando and so I knew that I could probably count myself as part of his huge Sherborne Ridout dynasty. However the test had only examined ten markers and so, by comparison with today's testing, the results were very non-specific but it was a start.

More recently the same member of my family, who I shall call Tom, submitted a cheek swab to one of the biggest DNA testing companies in the US, Family Tree DNA. I'd signed on the dotted line whilst I was at a family history show in London and for my money I was given a kit comprising a couple of sterile swabs, a container, labels and paperwork. I'd hoped that Tom's yDNA might connect us with more Ridouts and Rideouts around the world and perhaps make sense of our ancestry. I started an online Ridout yDNA project in the hope of furthering Orlando's quest of linking the Dorset Ridout families together.

The genetic material of the male Y chromosome (yDNA) remains fairly stable as it passes down the male line i.e. from grandfather to father to son, although some sections of the DNA strand are prone to mutations (changes) occasionally. Some short nucleotide sequences are replicated several times and these areas are known as short tandem repeats (STRs), or markers in the context of DNA testing; they mutate at a known frequency, some more often than others. If two men descend down different lines from the same distant male ancestor, their yDNA will probably have undergone a few of these mutations over successive generations. A statistician can compare the yDNA sequences of two men, noting which markers differ between them, and can estimate their relatedness i.e. how many generations back their common male ancestor (CMA) had probably lived. This is particularly useful if one or both men also have a paper trail of their family tree.

Many Ridouts in the US and Canada know that they descend from George Ridout (a baker and the son of Christopher Ridout, a miller (1669-1743) of Sherborne) and some may even have a family tree indicating how they are connected. Unfortunately, my tree is largely guesswork beyond the 1750's when I think my x4 great grandfather, John Ridout of Sherborne was born.

The recent 37 marker yDNA test, which my cousin Tom kindly submitted, has so far come quite close to matching two other Ridout men in my project;

one I will call Dick and the other Harry. Tom and Dick share 34/37 markers in common and Dick is a x6 great grandson of George Ridout; there is a 73% probability that Tom and Dick's CMA lived within 12 generations and an 89% probability that he lived within 16 generations and so I know that I do belong to this family somewhere.

Tom and Harry matched more closely to each other with 35/37 markers. Harry is a x3 great grandson of George Ridout. The statistics predict that Tom and Harry's CMA lived within 12 generations, with a 90% probability, and within 8 generations with a 70% probability. Harry and Dick descend down different lines from George Ridout: Dick from John Ridout (b. 1730, son of George and his first wife Mary HALLETT) and Harry from Thomas Ridout (b. 1754, son of George and his second wife Mary GIBBS). Not surprisingly, Dick and Harry's yDNA match 36/37 markers and the statistics correctly estimated their common ancestor to be within 8 generations with a 90% probability. Together, these data tell me that my ancestor is part of this tree, joining it at roughly the time frame of Christopher Ridout, his father or grandfather perhaps.

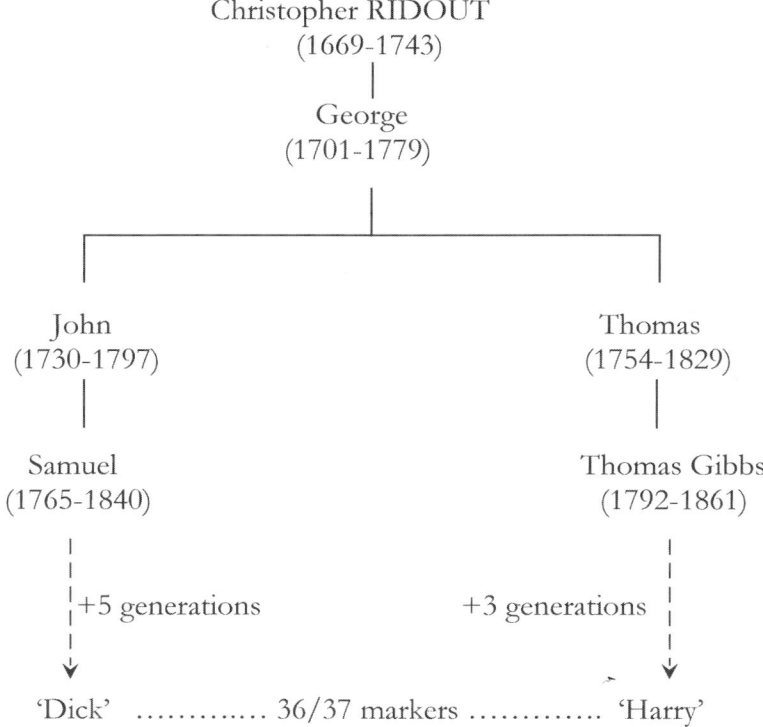

As a matter of record, my Ridout family's yDNA haplogroup is classified as SRY2627+ DYS490=10 DYS425=Null Type B (DYF371X=10c-10c-13c-14c) which, I am given to understand, is not common. A genetics project that focuses on SRY2627 gave me some background information: SRY2627 (also known as M167) was one of the first single nucleotide polymorphisms (SNPs) discovered in the human Y chromosome, back in 1997. It denotes a subgroup of haplogroup R1b1, the most common in Western Europe, currently (March 2013) classified as R1b1a2a1a1b5a by FTDNA or R1b1a2a1a1b1a2a1 by the International Society of Genetic Genealogy (ISOGG). M167 is not a large subgroup but is found particularly in places where R1b1 is very common - Iberia (especially the north and west i.e. the Basque Country and Catalonia), SW France and up the Atlantic coast to England, Wales, Ireland and Scotland. See also: http://en.wikipedia.org/wiki/Haplogroup_R1b1b2a1a2c_(Y-DNA).

4. William Ridowte of Hyle (1554[a]-1621)

Having established that my branch is part of the same family to which Christopher and George Ridout belong, I started my Sherborne research with the earliest known member of this clan, a man called William RIDOWTE (a variant spelling of Ridout[b]), who lived five generations earlier than George.

According to early research by Arthur Ridout [Ridout book, page 7], William Ridowte married a lady called Agneta (also Agnetha, or Agnes) BARNARD on the 15th October 1572 in Sherborne Abbey; parish records confirm this marriage. William was a yeoman, which Wikipedia defines as 'a free man holding a small landed estate, a minor landowner or a small prosperous farmer'. In other words, William was not working the land for the sole benefit of a manorial lord but had some measure of control over his own life, including the ability to move about the county without requiring permission to do so.

William and Agneta had two sons: Thomas born ~1574 and William born~1577. Agneta was buried in Sherborne on the 21st January 1619; William was buried on 30th June 1621 and, luckily for me, made a will (Fig. 5):

Figure 5: William Ridowte's will, 1620

I struggled to decipher a few of the words, the spelling is sometimes unfamiliar and the use of capital letters and punctuation do not of course conform to our modern convention. I did not see the original document but when in those days wills were recorded by a clerk, the contents were also copied into a book and these (copy wills) have survived in many cases. I have added a few commas here and there in the transcription to make it easier to read; any text in square brackets is my own…

"In the name of God Amen. The ninth day of May Ano Dm [AD] 1620, I William Ridowte the elder of Sherborne in the Countie of Dorset, yeoman, being sicke and weake of bodye but of sound and perfect memorie, God be praised for it, Doe ordaine and make this my last will and Testament in manner and forme following. ffirst I Commend my soule into the hands of Almighty god and my body to the earth in hope of glorious resurrection. And I will that my body be buried in my parish church of Sherborne aforesaid by the end of my seate there [he paid for a seat in the Abbey]. Unto the church of Sherborne aforesaid I give and bequeath sixe shillings eight pence. And to the poore of Sherborne aforesaid I give ten shillings. Item I give and bequeath to Mary Ridowt, daughter of my sonne Thomas Ridowte, twenty and seven pounds and one red cawled cowe [red coated cow] feeding and depastureing upon mine ground in Sherborne aforesaid. Item I give and bequeath to William Ridowte my godson, son of my said sonne Thomas Ridowte, ten pounds. Item I give and bequeath to Thomas Ridowte, Ambrose Ridowte and Walter Ridowte, children of the said Thomas Ridowte my sonne five pounds apiece. Item I give and bequeath to Robert Ridowte, Richard Ridowte, Julyan Ridowte and Agnes Ridowte children of the said Thomas my sonne four pounds apiece. Item I give and bequeath to my godson William Ridowte, son of my sonne William Ridowte, ten pounds and unto Thomas Ridowte, my sonne Williams son, also six pounds and unto Agnes, my son William his daughter, I give and bequeath twenty pounds. Also I give unto Johane Ridowte his daughter upon his second wife ffour pounds and to my servant Mary Richman twenty shillings. And I give to every of my godchildren twelve pence apiece. Item I give and bequeath to my sonne William Ridowte my musket, headpiece [helmet] and bandoleere [belt for carrying ammunition] and to my sonne Thomas I give my callyver [musket]. and unto my sonnes Thomas and William I freely forgive all such debts as they doe owe me further I will that my brewing pan do remain in my house to my sonne William during his life and afterwards to his son William Rydowte my godson forever. Item I give unto the foresaid Maria [Mary] Ridowte, my sonne Thomas his daughter, the standing bedstead and bed wherein I now lye together…. furniture to the same belonging and appertaining. And unto Agnes Ridowte, my son William Ridowte his daughter, I give my bedstead and bed… all furniture remaining in the lift over my chamber and wherein my mayden [maiden, possibly Mary Richman, his servant] do now lye. Item, I give to William Ridowte, Thomas Ridowtes son aforesaid, one cowe about three yeares of age now depasturing in the Moores in Sommerset [probably grazing on common land]. Item I give to Julyan

Ridowte, my sonne Thomas his daughter, a platter [plate] and a pottinger [porridge dish] and the chest that stands in my bedchamber I give to Marye Ridowte, my son Thomas his daughter. I give and bequeath unto my sonne Thomas Ridowte my lease of Cuffs tenement. Item I give and bequeath unto my son William Ridowte my lease of Hyle [lands that were part of the Hyle Farm estate in Sherborne] and all the yeares of and with same yet to come and all the cows in and upon the same now depasturing. Item I give unto Mary Ridowte, my son Thomas his daughter, my best cloke [cloak] and the second best cloke I give to Agnes Ridowte, my son Williams daughter, and to the said Mary, Thomas Ridowtes daughter, I give one brass pot and four platters and one candlestick, and one candlestick to Agnes Ridowte, William Ridowtes daughter, and one candlestick to Julyan Ridowte, Thomas Ridowtes daughter. Item I give unto the said Thomas Ridowte my sonne, one acre of barlie [barley] upon Palmers ground in Clanfield and one other ... upon the said Palmers ground in Haberfield and two acres of wheate upon Ridgewaie [Ridgeway]. I give and bequeath unto my sonne William one acre of wheat aboure Yuillewaie [Yuleway] being of high ground. To the said Thomas Ridowte and William Ridowte, my sons, I give and bequeath unto each of them a good cowe and one yearling calf bred by hand. I give unto Julyan, my sonne Thomas his daughter, and to Agnes his daughter I give two platters. The rest of my goods moveable and non moveable whatsoever not before given nor bequeathed I give and bequeath unto Agnes Ridowte, my son Thomas his daughter, whom I make my sole executrix of this my last will and testament and I do request my sonne Thomas Ridowte and my cousin John Hoddinott to be overseers of this my last will and testament and unto the said John Hoddinott I give ten shillings for his pain in that behalf. In witness whereof I have hereunto put my hand and seal the day and year above written, 1620."

The hand, mark and seal of William Ridowte Senr the testator, signed sealed and delivered to Thomas Ridowte one of the overseers to the use of the said Agnes Ridowte executrix in the presence of John Bealye. The sign of 'H' Agnes Ridowte, daughter of William Ridowte. The sign of 'A' Marie Ridowte. The sign of 'W' Edith Ridowte. The sign of Marie + [marked with a cross] Richman.

Today, in the US and Canada there may be thousands of William's descendants; a few hundred also live in the UK. Many of these people descend from Christopher Ridout of Sherborne who was probably one of the many x2 great grandsons of William Ridowte.

The will shows that William had a female servant, possessed firearms (which was usual for the time), a smallholding, two tenanted houses, livestock and crops; his estate was worth the equivalent of about £10,500 (in 2005). William's bequests helped me to draw the basis of his family tree.

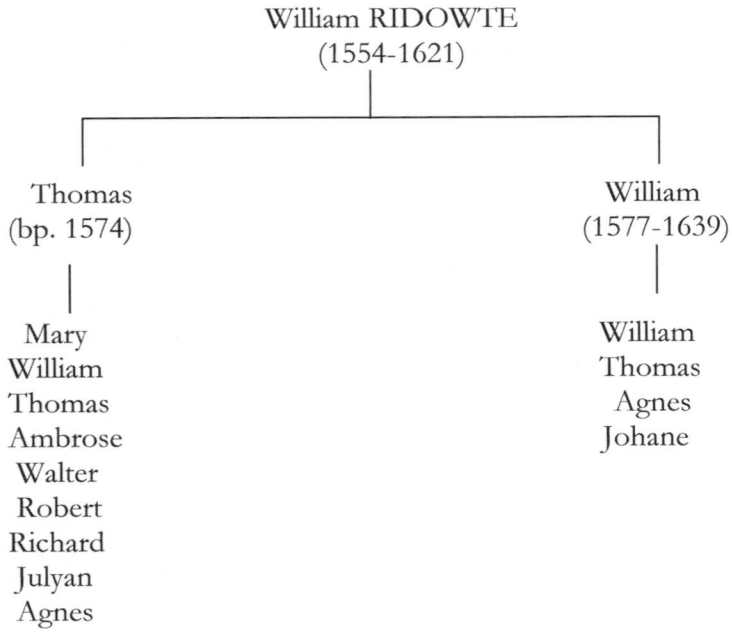

Footnotes:

a. William's birth year of 1554 is an approximation as he was said to be 60 years old when he was recorded as a tenant in a Sherborne Manor survey dated 1614. However, these documents were not always accurate (see Chapter 19).

b. During an era when many people could not read or write, those who were literate and kept records could only write down names as they heard them; the results can be interesting if the informant had a strong local accent!

5. Christopher Ridout of Henstridge (bp.1664): The Ridout Act

To genealogists and family historians from the United States of America and Canada, the name Christopher Ridout may be very familiar; in fact many of those folk regard this man as being their principal ancestor and will also know that Christopher married Mary GLOVER in Sherborne on 21st November 1697. What appears to be unclear in many minds, however, is just who Christopher actually was – so this is an introduction to not one but two Christophers.

Henstridge is a sizeable village in Somerset, about five miles ENE of Sherborne. This part of Somerset is still very rural and in the seventeenth century was mostly agricultural land and pasture, with a sprinkling of cottages and farms. In the village, the parish church of St Nicholas was probably where Christopher Ridout, son of Christopher Ridout of Henstridge and Edith (sometimes Judith) BLACKMORE of Hinton, was baptised on the 2nd November 1664 and where his parents had married seven years earlier.

Young Christopher's father and his Uncle William were both yeoman who held lands, tenements [houses] and messuages [dwelling houses with outbuildings and land] in nearby Horsington and Horsington Marsh, including a farm called Maltkiln Hill, which is still there today (Fig. 6, arrow).

When William died in 1669, he bequeathed his five year old nephew Christopher 'lands and grounds' called Even's Moor to be received when he was older and, of course, Christopher's father would also leave him his estate in due course. The boy grew up and, when he was seventeen, in anticipation of a union between him and John POPE's daughter, Christian, the two fathers drew up an agreement, on the 5th February 1680, by which lands and money changed hands in order to secure Christian's marriage portion [dowry]. Soon afterwards, Christopher and Christian married and had two boys, William (bp. 1683) and John (bp. 1685) but an unfortunate sequence of events then followed that would culminate in an Act of Parliament.

Firstly, Christopher Ridout's father died, leaving considerable debts, and then soon afterwards Christopher's son John died, then his wife Christian. Finally, at just thirty, Christopher himself died and was buried on the 14th

November 1694 leaving young William as the sole survivor of the family. Like his father, Christopher had borrowed sums of money and set up mortgages, probably quite a common practice in those days, but after his death his creditors couldn't claim their dues from his estate as legally it belonged to William, who of course was a minor.

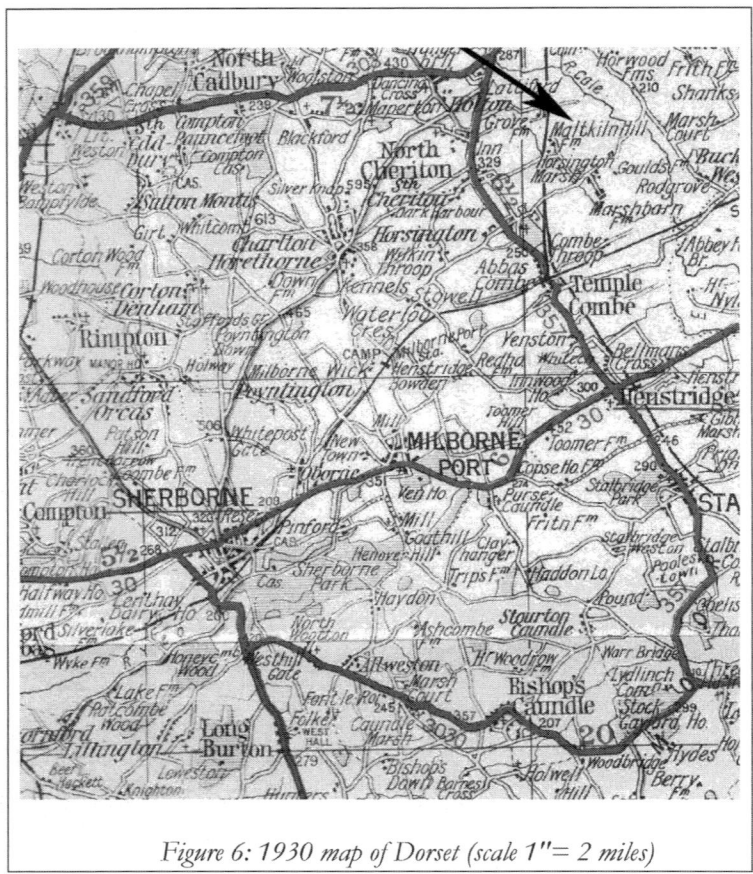

Figure 6: 1930 map of Dorset (scale 1"= 2 miles)

Parliament was petitioned and put into motion a Bill which went through both Houses in the spring of 1696 and finally received Royal Assent on the 10th April of that year.

The purpose of the Bill was to enable certain portions of Christopher's estate to be sold in order to pay his debts. Trustees were appointed and sold Maltkiln Hill Farm to Thomas Hussey of Horsington for £1,250. Hence the creditors were satisfied and at least some of the estate was preserved for

William, who would later become a haberdasher and a citizen of London. He died in 1736. A few years ago, I went to the House of Lords Archives and was allowed to handle, unroll and photograph the Ridout Bill (Fig. 7). It was an amazing experience. But, however interesting the story is, this Christopher is obviously not the man who married Mary Glover in 1697!

Figure 7: The Ridout Act (not original image)

On the 12th February 1669, in Sherborne Abbey, another Christopher Ridout, son of John and Elizabeth, was baptised. This man would live a long life, marry twice and have grandsons who would one day sail across the Atlantic to settle in the North American continent.

6. Christopher Ridout of Sherborne (bp.1669): The miller

Christopher Ridout, baptised on the 12th September 1669 in Sherborne Abbey, was one of eight children of husbandman [farmer] John Ridout and his wife Elizabeth. Arthur Ridout [Ridout book, page 63] recorded Elizabeth's maiden name as OLIVER but I couldn't find a marriage to support this. In 1678, John made his will (Fig. 8), the contents of which give some idea of his connection with the land. The following excerpts suggest that John's oldest son was William who, if legitimate, was no more than nineteen years old the year his father died; the will also names other children.

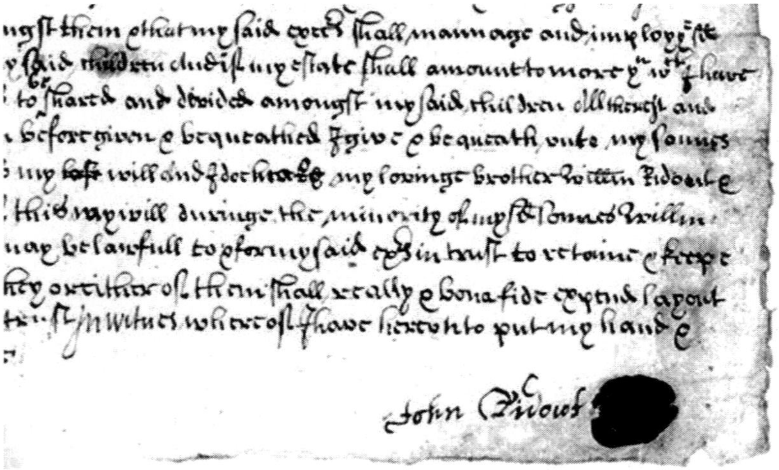

Figure 8: John Ridout's will, 1678

"*I give and bequeath unto my sonne William Ridout one wayne and wheels [wagon and wheels] one dunge pott [a manure wagon which tipped up for emptying] one sullow [plough] two yoaks two chaines and one pair of harrows… Item I give and bequeath unto my said son William Ridout one tenement with the appurtenances called Dollins and all my right estate title and interests of in, out, of and to the same he the said William paying yearly out of the same unto John, Richard, Christopher, Robert, Margaret and Frances, my sons and daughters, during the said term the yearly sum of twenty shillings apiece until they attain their several ages of one and twenty years and to be paid at two of the most usual feasts or terms of the year (that is to say) at Lady Day and Michaelmas by equal portions…*"

Figure 9: Sherborne Abbey

"Item I give unto my son John ten pounds. Item I give unto my daughter Julian five and twenty pounds. Item I give unto my daughter Margarett thirty pounds. I give unto my son Richard five and thirty pounds. Item I give unto my son Robert and to my daughter Frances forty pounds apiece all which legacies shall be paid unto my said sons when they shall attain their several ages of one and twenty years and unto my said daughters when they shall attain their several ages or date of marriage the which shall first happen…"

There are baptism records at Sherborne Abbey (Fig. 9) for John and Elizabeth's children, excepting William and Julian:

- 25th February 1660: John, son of John
- 26th December 1664: Margaret, daughter of John and Eliz
- 12th June 1667: Richard, son of John
- 12th September 1669: Christopher, son of John & Elizabeth
- 7th January 1670/1^c: Robert, son of John & Elizabeth
- 15th August 1675: Frances, daughter of John & Elizabeth

John's will continues…

"All the rest and residue my goods chattels lands and tenements not herein before given and bequeathed I give and bequeath to William and Robert who I make my executors of this my last will. And I do make my loving brother William Ridout and my brother in law Christopher Oliver executors in trust of this my will during the minority of my said sons William and Robert. And my will further is that it shall and may be lawful to and for my said executors in trust to retain and keep in their hands and custody so much money as they or either of them shall really and bone fide expend lay out or be put unto for or by reason of the said trust in witness where of I have here unto put my hand and seal the day and year first above written."

Interestingly, there is a marriage recorded in Sherborne of Christopher Oliver to Edith Ridout on the 24th October 1654. It is quite possible that Edith was John's sister and, if that were the case of course, John Ridout and Christopher Oliver would have been brothers-in-law, which means that John's wife Elizabeth may or may not also have been an Oliver. In Christopher Oliver's own will of 1688, an inventory of his possessions was prepared by, amongst others, a William Ridout who may have been the same 'loving brother' that John Ridout had mentioned.

To recap, Christopher Ridout's father John had a brother William (mentioned in Christopher Oliver's will) and maybe a sister Edith (who may have married Christopher Oliver). These relationships may prove to be important in establishing Christopher Ridout's connection back to William Ridowte of Hyle who, it is likely, was Christopher's great great grandfather.

Returning to Christopher's story... when he was eight, his mother Elizabeth died, and her death was followed a year later by that of his father John. Quite what happened to the young children we will never know but the next we hear of him, Christopher is twenty-five years old and marrying Mary PARSONS in Sherborne Abbey (24th June 1694). The Sherborne Ridout family had such a strong connection with this magnificent building which was their parish church and it was here that sadly, less than a year after their marriage, Christopher's wife was buried (24th May 1695) and Christopher married again to Mary Glover (21st November 1697).

Christopher appeared briefly in a manorial record dated 1695. The court leet, or view of frankpledge, was a court granted to a hundred, lordship, manor, or borough by the King's Charter. It was a form of self policing amongst the community such that about ten or so (male) householders formed a tithing which was held jointly responsible if one of its members committed an offence. Such matters would be brought before the hundred court and fines or imprisonment would be imposed, or perhaps the offender would be placed in the stocks. One of the court's concerns was 'to guard against all manner of encroachments upon the public rights, whether by unlawful enclosure or otherwise, to preserve landmarks, to keep watch and ward in the town, and overlook the common lands, adjust the rights over them, and restraining in any case their excessive exercise, as in the pasturage of cattle'. This court roll features both Christopher and William of Hyle.

(Court) Roll No 43 1695 North Wootton Tything. Thomas Ridout (probably the bailiff):

Court Leet held at Sherborne 13th April 1696. "We present William Ridout of Hile to amend his pitching at the ende of his orchard in Bow Lane by 24th May., sub poena 5d 'done'."

The residents of Westbury: Christopher Ridout on Jury for same; in Abbot Fee: Hayne Ryall, William Glover, William Collis, John Lambert, Richard Ridout; in Alweston: John

Fontleroy, Richard Ridout, tythingman (constable); Marsh Residents: John Ridout; Caundle Bishop: William Ridout; Haydon Tything: John Ridout; Bradford: Ambrose Ridout

Quite what the offence was is not clear – perhaps 'pitching' meant laying down a path but whatever it was, clearly a boundary was crossed and so William was fined five pence. Christopher appears to have represented the residents of Westbury, probably the area of Sherborne in which he lived. Note all the other Ridout men on this jury – possibly related, but the name was very common in Dorset, which certainly makes life complicated for any Ridout family historian!

Christopher and Mary had at least three children: John (baptised on the 4th July 1699), George (baptised on the 11th December 1701) and Elizabeth (baptised on the 19th July 1705). Throughout his life, Christopher and his family appeared several times in the Sherborne manor records, mainly through taking on leasehold or copyhold tenancies. The Lord of Sherborne Manor (Digby, Baron of 'Goatshill' i.e. Geashill in Ireland) had the freehold of the land and buildings thereon but would sell leases to tenants based on the term of lives; that is to say, a man might take out a lease on three lives – his own, his wife's and his son's – and when all three had eventually died, the property would revert back to the Lord. In the 17th Century, three lives might be considered the equivalent of our more modern 99 year lease. But, with the Lord's permission, and on payment of a 'fine', lives were often exchanged throughout the lifetime of the property. This system enabled a family to keep their tenancies on a fairly long term basis and, as they gradually moved up in the world, take on more property. In this way a man could eventually farm a good deal of land, progressing from a husbandman to a yeoman, maybe purchasing his own copyhold land.

Every now and again, the Lord of the Manor would conduct a survey of his lands and the resulting documents show the names of his tenants, their properties, rents and herriotts (payment due on the death of the tenant). Christopher appeared four times in the Sherborne Manor Survey of 1709; he appeared to have two tenancies in Eastbury, one in Primsley tithing and one in Gilland – areas of Sherborne.

The reference to property in Primsley is interesting as this area bordered the Hyle Farm estate (where William Ridowte, Christopher's x2 great grandfather, had farmed land), close to the River Yeo (Fig. 10). West Mill (arrow) fell within Primsley and at some point in his life Christopher Ridout became a miller.

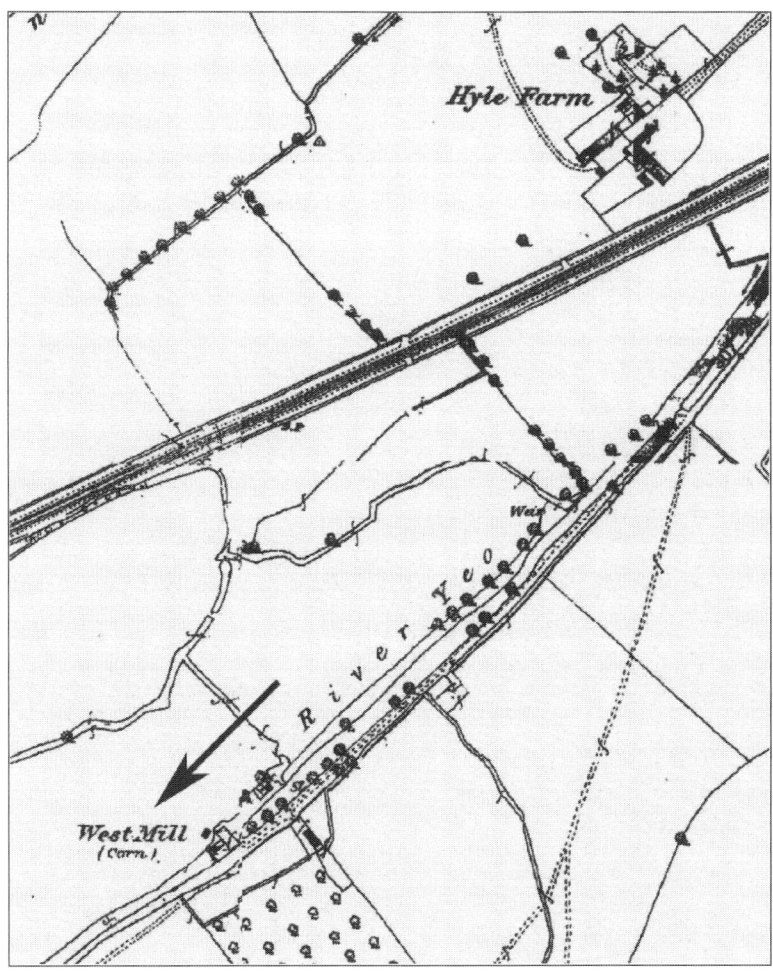

Figure 10: Hyle Farm and West Mill, 1887

Footnote:

c. Before 1752, we used the Julian calendar whereby the year started on March 25th (Lady Day). This meant that January 1st to March 24th was at the end of the year, not the beginning. This was often expressed as a double date e.g. 7th January 1670/71, which would mean January 1671 by our modern convention.

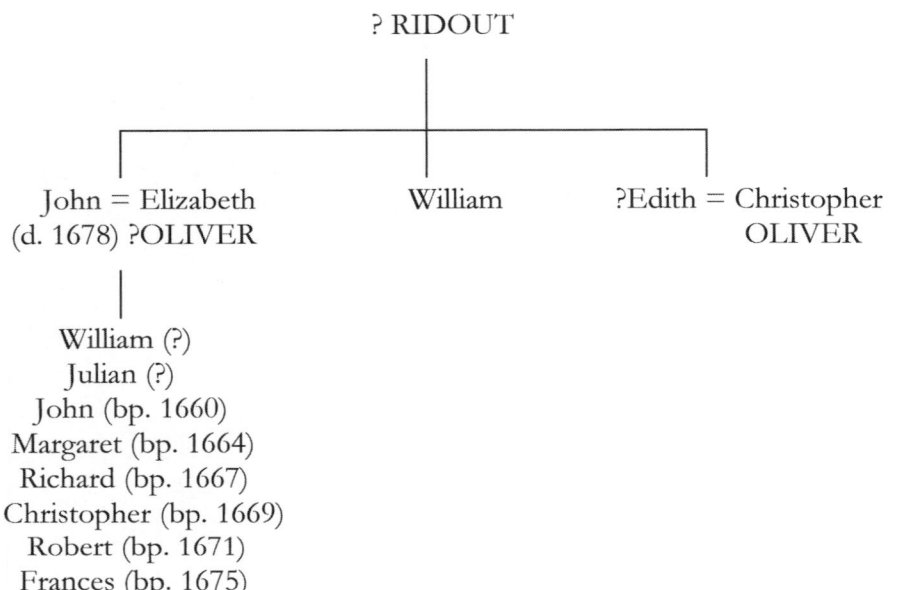

7. Hyle Farm, Limekiln Farm and Ridout's Mill

As discussed in the last chapter, Christopher Ridout was mentioned in the 1709 survey when he was forty years old; he was an assignee of Thomas Hobbs, a gentleman, who had the lease of Primsley Farm from the Lord of the Manor, William Lord Digby. This lease was for a term of lives where the 'lives' were Thomas Hobbs, Anne his wife and Mary Napper (daughter of Samuel Napper). The property in question was two acres of land, part of the Primsley Farm estate, comprising a house, garden, orchard and backside (yard at the rear of the house) which were on a street called Westbury; also about eleven acres of meadow land called Raw Meade.

By 1720, Thomas Hobbs had died and the property reverted back to Lord Digby who, on 26th July, leased it out to Christopher Ridout, miller and Thomas Loaden, baker both of Sherborne, for a payment of £62-6s-0d. The lives were amended to include Elizabeth, Christopher's daughter.

In 1735, Christopher still held this lease, together with Thomas Ridout (relationship unknown). The 'lives' were Mary Fox (née Napper, now a widow), Rebecca Loaden and Elizabeth Ridout. Presumably Anne Hobbs had also died. Interestingly, a separate moiety of Primsley Farm had been re-named Limekiln; Limekiln Farm exists today and is not far away from Hyle Farm.

Christopher died in 1743 and was buried in Sherborne on the 1st June. Intriguingly, the entry in the parish register states 'Christopher Ridout from workhouse was buried'. As there is no suggestion that Christopher was destitute, a possible explanation is that the workhouse also functioned as a hospital in which he may well have been a patient. He had written his will less than a month before dying (Fig 11):

"By this my last Will and Testament made this seventh day of May one thousand and seven hundred and forty three, I Christopher Ridout of Sherborne in the County of Dorset Yeoman do give and dispose of my worldly Goods and Estate in manner and fform following that is to say In the first place I give devise and bequeath unto Mary my loving wife all that my piece of land lying in the common ffields of Sherborne aforesaid containing about One acre & halfe & now in the possession of John Lukus with the appurtenances thereto belonging To hold to my said wife and to the Heirs and Assigns forever. Also all the rest and residue of my

Real and personal estate whatsoever and wheresoever the same do lye and whereof I shall die seized or possessed or any way intituled unto. And also all singular my Goods Chattles & Credits after payment of my just Debts and Funeral expenses I give devise and bequeath unto my said wife Mary and to her Heirs Executors Admon and Assigns respectively. And I do hereby make constitute and appoint my said Wife Mary sole executrix of this my last Will and Testament hereby revoking all former and other Wills by me at any time heretofore made. In Witness whereof I the said Christopher Ridout have hereunto sett my Hand and Seal the Day and Year above written."

This Will was proved at Sarum on the 4th July 1743 before the Reverend John Talman Clerk M.A. Lawful Surrogate of the Official of the Dean of Sarum.

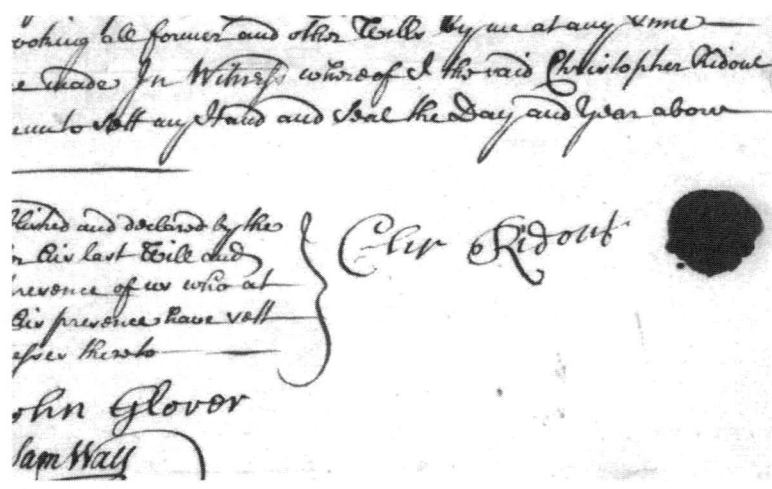

Figure 11: Christopher Ridout's signature, 1743

In the 1748 Sherborne Manor estates survey, the moiety of Primsley Farm was entered under Christopher's assigns and hence his widow Mary and son George remained lives on the tenancy and may also have occupied the property. George also had a tenancy of Little Raw Mead, five acres of meadowland nearby for which he was granted the lease ten years later by Lord Digby.

The various Sherborne Manor surveys, contracts and accounts make it clear that whilst William Ridout had a tenancy at Hyle, first Christopher and then his son George had tenancies in the neighbouring tithing of Primsley Manor. Modern maps still show Hyle Farm and Limekiln Farm but where was the mill in which Christopher then George worked? Here I think, is the answer….

According to documents held by the Dorset Record Office, a silk-throwing business was established in 1753 by John SHARRER, a London silk-thrower, who leased Westbury Mill and built a new mill-house. Westbury Mill was clearly shown in the revised 1901 OS map of the area but has long since been used for other purposes and these days is referred to as the Old Yarn Mill; its location is just across the road from Hyle Farm.

An indenture between Lord Digby and John Sharrer incidentally makes reference to Ridout's Mill and indicates that it was almost certainly what was later called West Mill…

"This indenture made the second day of April in the twenty eighth year of the reign of our sovereign Lord George the Second by the Grace of God of Great Britain France and Ireland King Defender of the Faith and in the year of Our Lord one thousand seven hundred and fifty five between the Right Honourable Edward Lord Digby and Henry Digby Esquire his brother of the one part and John Sharrer of Little Aycliffe Street Goodman's Fields London silk thrower of the other part. Whereas the said Edward Lord Digby by his indenture of lease bearing the date the day next before the day of the date hereof in consideration of the sum of fifty pounds of lawfull money of Great Britain therein mentioned to be paid him by the said John Sharrer hath demised granted and to farm letten unto the said John Sharrer all that water grist mill, dwelling house, garden, orchard, barn, backsides, parrocks and parcels of ground adjoining the said mill and barn and one plot of meadow or pasture ground <u>lying near a lane leading to a mill called Ridouts mill</u> and one acre of meadow ground lying in the upper moore all which said premises are situate lying and being in the homage of Westbury in the manor of Sherborne in the county of Dorset and now in the possession of the said John Sharrer together with all and singular mill ponds, mill pool, mill dams, streams, water courses, ways, paths, passages, easements, profits, commons, commodities and appurtenances whatsoever to the said mill and premises belonging or in anywise appertaining (except as therein is mentioned to be excepted)…."

The date on which the Ridout family took possession of the mill is unknown. On 16th Century maps, it was labelled Cooth's or Couthe's Mill, suggesting an earlier leaseholder. West Mill still stands (Fig. 12) although it sadly dilapidated but there are faint hopes that it can be restored. Maybe once again it will churn the waters of the Yeo, perhaps drive the grinding gear that once made the corn flour that made the bread that George baked. His business made him wealthy enough to send his sons and daughters into the world where some made their names such that houses, streets and towns in the American sub-continent were named after them. To distant Ridouts, this is your heritage - a little Dorset watermill.

Figure 12: Ridout's Mill (West Mill), Sherborne

An interesting postscript to this story is that one of John Sharrer's nephews, who went into the business in Westbury Mills (being a silk throwster) was George WARD, a man who subsequently married George Ridout's daughter Elizabeth on the 15th February 1768 in Sherborne.

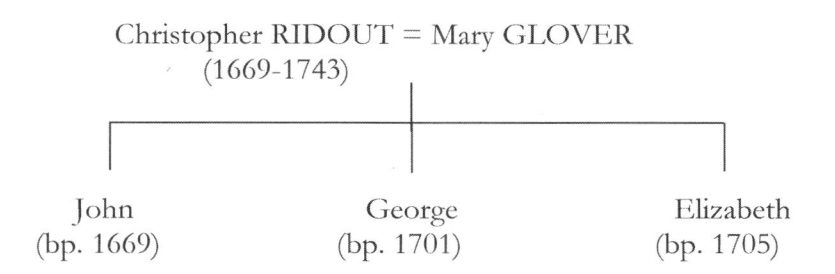

```
            Christopher RIDOUT = Mary GLOVER
                  (1669-1743)
         ┌───────────────────┼───────────────────┐
       John                George              Elizabeth
     (bp. 1669)          (bp. 1701)           (bp. 1705)
```

8. Linking William of Hyle and Christopher Ridout

Christopher Ridout, miller and yeoman of Sherborne, son of John and Elizabeth Ridout, was undoubtedly a descendant of William Ridowte of Hyle, but in decades of research by different individuals it has been difficult to determine the exact lineage between William and Christopher. Genealogy often involves building up a hypothesis and then trying to shoot it down in flames; if a theory cannot be disproved then it stands, with provisos. This is my theory and it is a little complicated and so I have used numbered superscripts to identify particular individuals (see also the tree diagram at the end of this chapter).

When William Ridowte of Hyle died in 1621 (Chapter 4), two sons survived him: Thomas[1] who was baptised on the 12th April 1574 and William[1] who was baptised on the 11th May 1577, both in Sherborne Abbey.

Thomas[1] married twice. By his first wife, Edith OLDISH, he had five children – one of them was Thomas[2] (bp. 10th October 1601) and another William[2] (bp. 28th November 1599). William[1] also married twice. By his first wife, Margaret POPE, he had four children – one of them was William[3] (bp. 13th December 1602). So, there were two boys named William, who were first cousins. On the 3rd February 1622/3 in Sherborne Abbey, the Williams married two sisters in a double event. Thomas[1]'s son William[2] married Julyan TOOGOOD and William[1]'s son, William[3], married Ann Toogood. These unions probably cemented relations between the two families, which was probably very useful in terms of land and property, but a nightmare when it came to sorting out 17th century baptisms! Sisters Julyan and Ann were daughters of William Toogood and his wife Joan (née CUFF). Joan left a will in 1629 as did another daughter of hers, Magdalen Toogood. These and other documents helped me to slot the various Ridout families together.

In his appraisal of this family conundrum, Victorian genealogist Arthur Ridout 'married' William[3] to Julyan Toogood, not Ann [Ridout book, page 9; corrected by Bill Ridout on page 9a] and also credited William[3] with a long life and many children. However William[3] actually died as a young man, in July 1630; his widow Ann married Robert PARFITT on the 3rd May 1635. Whilst it is certain that Ann (bp. 20th June 1624), and probably William (bp. 8th April

1627) were born of William³ and Ann, other children baptised in Sherborne to a 'William Ridout', including Thomas (bp. 1st January 1623/4), Julian (bp. 26th July 1628) and Margaret (bp. 9th February 1629/30), probably did not belong to this couple.

As soon as I found William³'s death in 1630 it seemed unlikely that this man was Christopher Ridout's grandfather, because the only John 'son of William' was baptised on the 4th May 1634. Although not impossible, it seems odd that Ann waited four years to baptise her late husband's son child: I think that this baptism might relate to John, the son of William² and his wife Julyan.

Various manorial records suggest that Christopher's father John was born in ~1632 and the nearest baptism in Sherborne parish records was on the 24th February 1630/1, 'John Rideout, son of Thomas'. Although it can't be proved conclusively, this may well have been son of Thomas² and his wife Eleanor.

Christopher appears to have been a great great grandson of William Ridout of Hyle either through William² or Thomas². With the benefit of more information, I re-visited this issue a few months later and concluded that William² and Julyan were actually the more likely parents of this John Ridout (see Chapter 15).

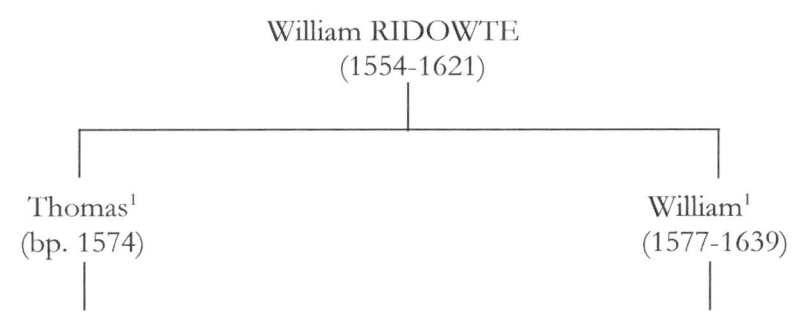

William RIDOWTE
(1554-1621)

Thomas¹ (bp. 1574)   William¹ (1577-1639)

William² (bp. 1599) = Julyan* → John (bp. 1634)   William³ (bp. 1602) = Ann*
Thomas² (bp. 1601) = Eleanor → John (bp. 1631)

* TOOGOOD sisters

9. George Ridout (1701-1779): baker of West Mill

Christopher Ridout's second son was George (1701-1779). When he grew up, George was by trade a baker and probably succeeded to his father's business at West Mill. The mill had originally been built in the sixteenth century but was apparently re-built in about 1730, perhaps by Christopher or George?

George married his first wife, Mary HALLETT, on 25th November 1725 at Milborne Port in Somerset. The couple had several children including:

- George (bp. 24th November 1726): a baker like his father. Married Hester TRIMNELL; the couple had no children.
- Mary (bp. 4th March 1726/7): married John HODDINOTT of Sherborne, an upholsterer.
- John (bp. 16th March 1729/30): went to Oxford University (1749-1753) from where he went directly to America as secretary to Horatio SHARPE, Governor of Maryland. He married Mary, a daughter of Governor Samuel OGLE; the couple lived at Ridout House, Annapolis, which he had built in 1765 (Fig. 13).
- Edith (bp. March 1733): died the year of her birth.
- Nicodemus (bp. 12th July 1734): married Betty CHAR(M)BURY. One of their sons, George, went to Toronto and was, for a time justice of the peace. Nicodemus was a merchant and burgess who settled and died in Bristol, Gloucestershire.
- Samuel (bp. 24th September 1735): died the year of his birth.
- Edith (bp. 22nd September 1737): married Isaac FINCH of London, a hatter.
- Elizabeth (bp. 29th November 1739): married George WARD silk throwster and had at least seven children including sons John Sharrer Ward and George Ridout Ward.

Mary died on the 9th December 1751 and George married a second time on the 15th May 1753 at Long Burton, Dorset to Mary GIBBS, a lady fifteen years his junior. The couple had two sons:

- Thomas (bp. 17th March 1754): went to America in 1774 and had several adventures, including being captured by a party of Shawnee, of which much is written. Moved on to Canada and became Surveyor General in Toronto and was elected to the Legislature in 1812. Married twice and had a great many children, some of whom became prominent in Canadian society.

- John Gibbs (bp. 24th June 1757): stayed in London and became an eminent doctor. Married Elizabeth HOLMES and had six children.

Figure 13: Ridout House, Annapolis, c. 1930

Here are two letters of interest; they are lodged with the Ridout Collection in the Society of Genealogists in London…

Over Stowey, 8th January 1888, from Susan Ward (granddaughter of Elizabeth Ridout and George Ward) to her cousin Frances Ward of Longbridge Deverill near Warminster…

"I am quite certain that our grandmother Elizabeth Ward (née Ridout) was whole sister to the Ridout who went out to America to be secretary to the Governor of Maryland. I used to hear my Father mention the name of the Governor but do not remember it and don't know Mr Ridout's Christian name; he went straight from college to America. The Governor of Maryland wrote to his friend the Head of the College asking him to send out a young man whom he could highly recommend. This must have occurred some years before the war of

Independence which began 1775 and the Independence was declared 1782. Our Grandmother did not go out with him but went as a guest later on: I think she was with him some little time before she resolved to throw in her lot with him – she returned to England to take leave of her relations but the war breaking out she was obliged to alter her plans and our Grandfather (George Ward) becoming her suitor, she married and settled down in the old land. It is not likely Mr Ridout was less than 20 when he was sent after doing well at College and he must have been in America six years before the war: I believe his sister was with him three years. She used to be very proud of telling us how she danced a minuet in Washington's House, Franklyn playing the musical glasses for the dancers. The Tom Ridout who wrote the long letter giving an account of his adventures in Canada in 1789 was half brother of our grandmother – so was Dr Ridout. Miss Mary Ridout was a far off cousin of his but considered herself more nearly connected with some Miss Ridouts who were living at Sherborne. Our grandmother died aged 86 – was living in 1825 probably 1826."

From George Ridout Ward [son of Elizabeth Ridout and George Ward] found by his daughter Frances and forwarded to a relative from Sandhurst on 10th July 1884…

"Christopher Ridout, miller of Sherborne and also farmer, lived at Ridout's Mill and married a Miss Glover. They had three children John, George and Elizabeth. John went to America in consequence of a disappointment in love but it is supposed he married in America. Mr John Ridout (son of George), going to America some years afterwards lodged at a widow's house in New York of the name Ridout and it was supposed by his father she must have been the widow of his son^d *John. Her husband's name was John and he told her that he came from a town in the west of England, but would not tell her the name. He came to England as master of a trading vessel but never visited his parents. He once sent for his brother to Bristol and saw him but declined to see his parents.*

George married Mary Hallett daughter of Nicodemus Hallett of Milborne Port – he possessed a respectable leasehold property on which he lived. George and Mary Ridout lived at Ridout's Mill, the said George Ridout succeeding to his father's mill & property. George and Mary Ridout had eight children: George, Mary, John, Edith (died), Nicodemus, Edith, Samuel and Elizabeth. George died without issue and was a baker. Mary married J Hoddinott of Sherborne, upholsterer by whom she had three children: John & Mary who died and James who married and left one daughter. John went to America, secretary to Governor Sharpe of Maryland and married Miss Ogle the succeeding Governor's daughter by whom he had three children: Samuel, Horatio and Anne. Samuel married a Miss Addison, descended from the writer of the Spectator and was a judge. Horatio lived on his own property. Anne married a Mr Gibson, a merchant. Nicodemus lived at Bristol, a maltster He married twice and had families. Edith married Mr Finch a draper in London and had a son who died and

Elizabeth, a daughter who married Mr Scudamore. Elizabeth married George Ward, silk throwster of Sherborne, son of George Ward of Sawbridgeworth in Hertfordshire and they had children: John Sharrer Ward, Susannah Ward, George Ridout Ward, Elizabeth Ward who married Woollam, Mary Ward, who married Burges and Thomas Ward."

George Ridout Ward, son of Elizabeth Ridout and George Ward wrote that his grandparents and great grandparents lived at the mill. I wondered how that might be possible since when I saw West Mill on a visit to Sherborne; it looked too small and would have been filled with the grinding machinery and totally unsuitable for human habitation. However, this matter was clarified by the curator of Sutton Poyntz Water Museum who has apparently researched West Mill and so I was lucky enough to receive some information about the fabric of the building: "It was built of local rubble stone, three floors high with a roof of stone slats and standing on sloping ground such that on the upstream side, the stone floor could be entered by a doorway nearly at ground level. There was a miller's cottage joined to the right of the building, behind which was the bakery." The cottage was demolished long ago.

It seems likely that three generations of this family lived at what was then known as Ridout's Mill; I know they were in possession at least by 1720 and that they relinquished the business and the building after George's death, as a newspaper advertisement shows (Fig. 14).

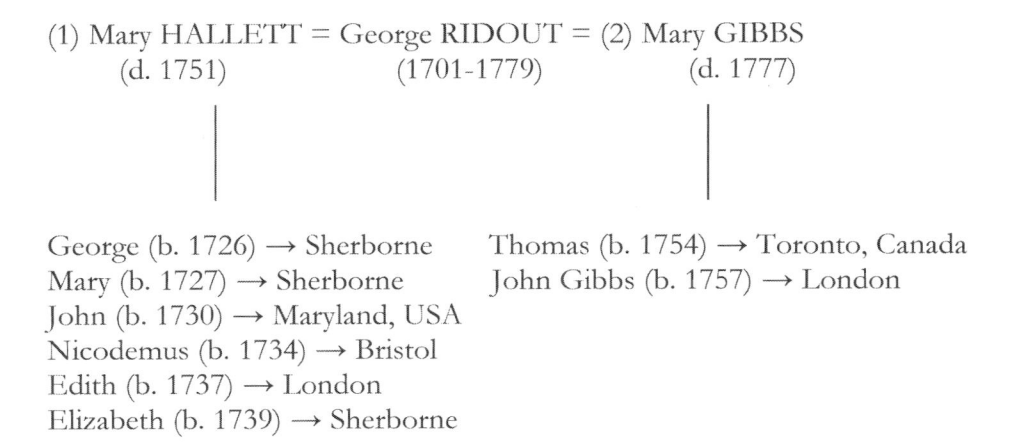

(1) Mary HALLETT = George RIDOUT = (2) Mary GIBBS
    (d. 1751)   (1701-1779)   (d. 1777)

George (b. 1726) → Sherborne   Thomas (b. 1754) → Toronto, Canada
Mary (b. 1727) → Sherborne   John Gibbs (b. 1757) → London
John (b. 1730) → Maryland, USA
Nicodemus (b. 1734) → Bristol
Edith (b. 1737) → London
Elizabeth (b. 1739) → Sherborne

Footnote:

d. George's son John went to America in 1753. His grandfather Christopher died in 1743 and couldn't have expressed an opinion on whether or not the mysterious Mrs Ridout was the widow of his son. It is more likely that John's father George would have guessed at Mrs Ridout's identity, in which case this should perhaps read *"she must have been the widow of his brother"* not of his father.

> Sherborne, May 8, 1780
>
> TO be SOLD by AUCTION, (together or in separate lots) by JAMES HODDINOTT, on Thursday the 15th June next at the Half Moon inn in the town, between the hours of two and six in the afternoon, unless sooner disposed of by private contract, of which notice will be given in this paper.
>
> All that Water Grist and Flour Mill and Malt-house, which has been lately new-built, known by the name of RIDOUT'S MILL, being well supplied with water and every other convenience, together with two closes thereunto adjoining called THE HAMMS, containing about two acres; likewise three acres of good orchard ground, planted with the best fruit-trees, now in its prime; and also one close called HUNGERHILL, containing about six acres of good arable ground: All now let for the remainder part of a lease, of which ten years are yet to come at the yearly rental of 31l. 10s. with a covenant from the tenant to keep the premises in repair.
>
> Also a Close of Meadow called LONGMEAD, containing about four acres, and now let at 9l. per annum, to a tenant at will.
>
> All of which said premises are now held for the remainder of a term of 99 years determinable on two good lives.
>
> Also one close of meadow called LITTLE BERNARD's LEASE, containing about five acres, and now let at 9l. 12s. per annum. For the remainder part of a lease of which five years yet are to come.
>
> Which two closes are now held for the remainder of a term of 99 years, determinable on three good lives.
>
> All persons having any claim or demand on the estate and effects of the late Mr. George Ridout are desired to deliver in an account thereof to Mr. John Melmoth, school-master in Sherborne. Also, any persons indebted to the said estate and effects are desired to pay the same to Mr. George Ward of Bruton, Mr. Nic. Ridout in Milk-street, Bristol, executors of the said Mr. George Ridout, or to the aforesaid Mr. J. Melmoth, whom they have authorised to receive the same, and of whom further particulars may be known.

Figure 14: Sherborne Mercury, 1780. Sale of Ridout's Mill

10. Exploding the myth: Huguenot Ridouts!

Figure 15: Thomas Ridout

To recap: George Ridout, the miller and baker of Sherborne (1701-1779) married twice. By his first wife Mary HALLETT, he had many children, including John (1730-1797) and by his second wife, Mary GIBBS, George had two more sons, one of whom was Thomas (1754-1829). John went to America in 1753 and half brother Thomas followed him in 1774. John settled in Annapolis, Maryland, married a governor's daughter and was a close friend and personal secretary of Governor Horatio Sharpe, a relationship which would one day see John owning Sharpe's thousand acre estate and house at Whitehall in Annapolis, MD.

Thomas Ridout (Fig. 15) initially went to Annapolis too but, after many adventures, he moved and settled in Canada in 1788 and held many prestigious positions in his time including Sergeant-at-Arms to the House of Assembly in 1794, Surveyor General of Upper Canada in 1810 and Member of Parliament in 1812. Married twice, Thomas had many children including George (1791-1871) and Thomas Gibbs (1792-1861).

At the age of nineteen, young Thomas Gibbs Ridout (Fig. 16) sailed across the sea to England to seek his fortune if opportunity presented itself. He wrote many letters to his father and brother George during his travels including an interesting diary entry, dated Sunday 9th February 1812, concerning a brief visit to Sherborne, Dorset – his ancestral home.

"On my visit to Sherborne, I went to see my old grandfather's house. I found it in ruins, the hedges are out of repair, and the avenue of trees leading to the house have their tops cut off. I also went to see the grammar school, which now consists of twenty boys, kept by Rev. J. Cutler. It was Christmas holidays. A girl came out and civilly unlocked the door. I walked up and down the room, saw the oaken benches, desks and wainscoting cut up and carved with 3,000 names; saw John Gibbs Ridout carved upon one. I went to Sherborne church on Sunday, sat just below the fine old organ, and had a full view of the grandeur of this Gothic pile, which has stood unmoved in war and peace, through the storms and tempests of 700 years, its clustered pillars forming a lofty, deep arch. The mossy walls seem to defy time, and I think that seven centuries may again roll away, and this building will remain in a perfect state. After church, James Ridout showed me grandfather's seat, near the pulpit, which I entered—the place beyond Lord Digby's. There, on that spot, fifty years ago, sat my father, in the other corner, grandfather. Here in this church, for generations, had the family been christened and buried; but I found myself more a stranger in Sherborne than any other town I had been in. James Ridout, being churchwarden, showed me the parish books from 1640. In 1630 I saw the name of John Ridout in the vestry."

This passage and many others of interest are to be found in a volume entitled 'Ten Years in Upper Canada: Peace and War 1805-1815' having been collated and annotated by Matilda (Ridout) Edgar, daughter of Thomas Gibbs Ridout and wife of Sir James D Edgar. The volume was published in 1890. Lady Edgar also wrote a book called 'A Colonial Governor in Maryland 1753-1773', published in 1912. It is the story of Horatio Sharpe, as Governor of Maryland, a position which he took up in 1753 having travelled from his native Yorkshire taking with him young John Ridout, as his secretary.

Figure 16: Thomas Gibbs Ridout

I enjoyed reading both of these books but I was surprised to read the following passage in the latter volume:

"John Ridout, the youngest of the trio, was born at Sherborne, Dorsetshire, England, in 1732, and was therefore but twenty-one years old when he arrived in Maryland. He had just graduated at the University of Oxford after five years' residence there, and had been recommended for the position of secretary by his Hebrew professor to Dr. Gregory Sharpe, who had been commissioned by his brother the governor to find him 'a scholar and a gentleman' to accompany him to America. That the place of secretary was no sinecure the voluminous correspondence preserved in the archives of Maryland bears witness. Of Huguenot descent, for the Ridouts had left France in the sixteenth century, presumably on account of the religious persecutions in that country, John Ridout was throughout his life firm in his convictions, straightforward in his conduct and, as became his ancestry, somewhat austere. He soon won the esteem and affection of Governor Sharpe, whose letters bear testimony to the worth of his young secretary."

There was also the following footnote, information acknowledged by Lady Edgar as having been provided to her by Dr William Govane Ridout of Annapolis, great grandson of John Ridout:

"The Ridouts (spelt also Rideout) of Sherborne, were descendants of Thomas Ridout of Henstridge, Somerset. The family came originally from France from the neighbourhood of Fontainebleau and settled in England about the middle of the sixteenth century. In Hutchins' Visitation of Somerset, now in the College of Arms, London, mention is made of the granting of a coat-of-arms in 1551 to Thomas Ridout of Henstridge. These arms bear a striking resemblance to those borne by the de Rideouts de Sance (see Hozier's Armorial General of the French Nobility), near Fontainebleau. In the will of Walter Ridout of Langlin, Dorset, a descendant of Thomas, dated 1582, among other legacies he bequeaths a large sum of money to the church at Fontainebleau. Christopher Ridout, son of Thomas, was baptized at Henstridge, Somerset, 24th November 1664, and settled in Sherborne, Dorset. His eldest son, George, born at Sherborne in 1702, was the father of the John Ridout who came to America with Horatio Sharpe."

Appearing as it does in such a well written and researched book, this paragraph has probably led many Sherborne Ridout descendants to think that their ancestors were French Huguenots. As a Ridout family historian, I think I should at least provide some alternative information so that interested parties might make their own judgements although I know that some myths are hard to dispel.

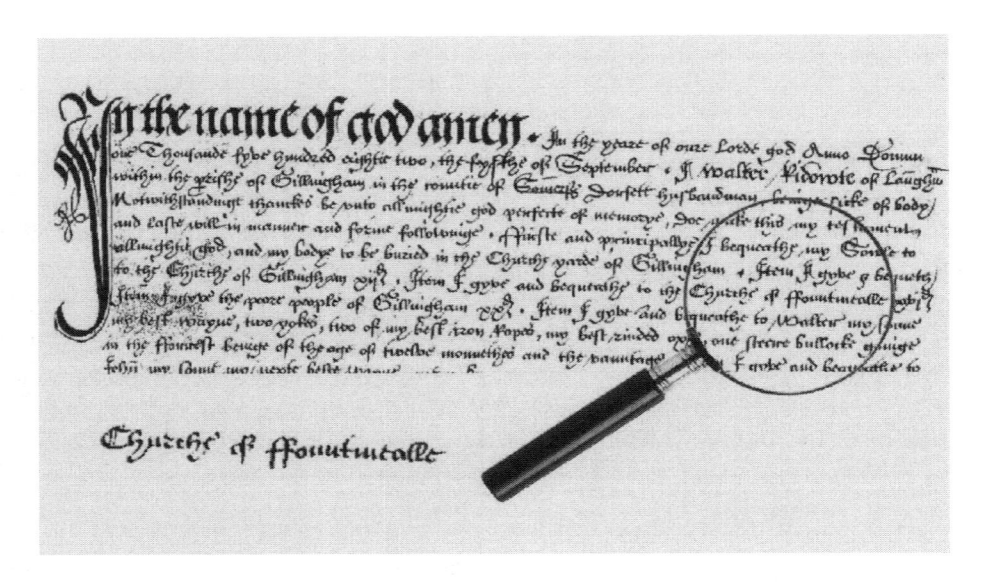

Figure 17: Walter Ridout's bequest to Fontmell church, 1582

The two points I offer in evidence are these. Firstly, as already discussed in Chapter 6, George Ridout the baker was son of Christopher Ridout of Sherborne (bp. 1669) NOT Christopher Ridout of Henstridge (bp. 1664). Secondly, an examination of the will of Walter Ridout of Langham, Gillingham, dated 5th September 1582 (Fig. 17), shows that he made a bequest not to a church in Fontainebleu, France but to the parish church of ffountmealle, which is an archaic spelling of Fontmell – as in Fontmell Magna, in Dorset. The 'large sum of money' was 16d! The reason that Walter remembered the church in his will was probably because his father, the Rev. William Ridout, had been the rector in Fontmell Magna from 1549 to 1554; he was persecuted for his religious views during the reign of the Catholic Queen Mary.

11. John Ridout of Sherborne to John Ridout of Bath

Over the years I have spent a great deal of time researching several Ridout lines, although my own seems the hardest to trace. A comparison of yDNA sequences between various Ridout males has shown that my family is matched with known descendants of Christopher Ridout of Sherborne (Chapter 3). The statistics suggest that our common male ancestor might have lived roughly between 1652 and 1712.

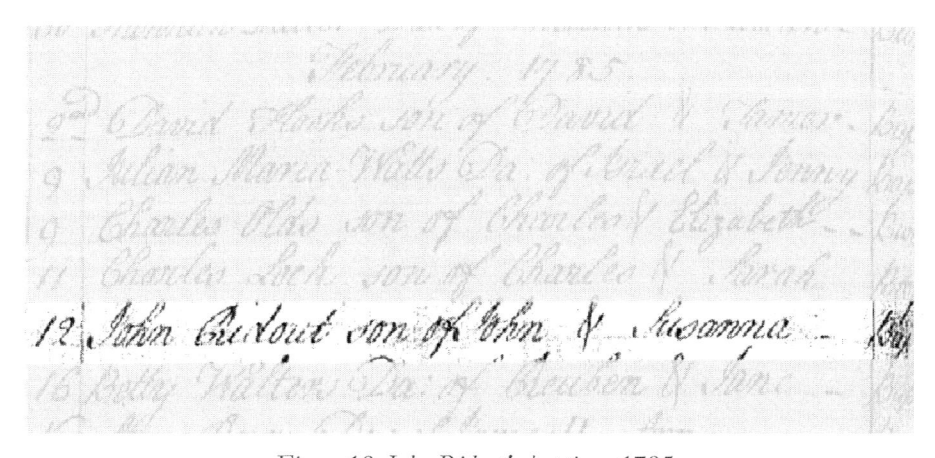

Figure 18: John Ridout's baptism, 1785

To recap: John Ridout, my x3 great grandfather, was baptised in Sherborne on 12th February 1785 (Fig. 18). His parents were John and Susanna Ridout; the couple also had other children between 1783 and 1796. The only marriage that I could find was that of John Ridout and Susanna Shore at Sherborne Abbey on Sunday 5th August 1781. Although there were two other 'John and Susanna' pairings in Dorset at a similar time (one in Purse Caundle and the other in Gillingham), following these families forward in time led to their elimination.

The burials in Sherborne of two John Ridouts: one on the 11th December 1826, aged 76 and another on the 25th April 1827, aged 73; also a Susanna Ridout on the 3rd March 1817, aged 65 gives rough estimates of birth years, if indeed any of these were my x4 great grandparents. After years of searching, the only Susanna Shore I have found was baptised on May 6th 1755, daughter of James and Ann Shore at Haselbury Plucknett (about 12 miles from Sherborne).

When John and Susanna married in 1781 (Fig. 19) neither party could sign their name, which was not uncommon in those days. Witness William Ridout, also 'made his mark'; perhaps he was John's brother. On Christmas Day 1779 in Sherborne Abbey, William Ridout married Ann Andrews and his witnesses were John Ridout & Sarah Ridout; all three made their mark. Were John and Sarah husband and wife or brother and sister, in which case were they siblings of William? I'll never know for certain.

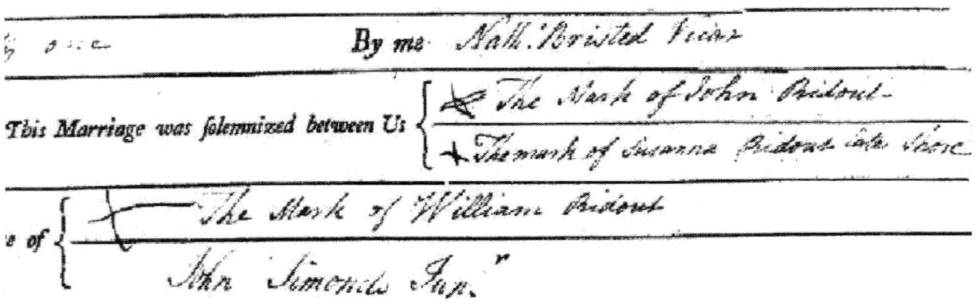
By me Nath. Bristed Vicar

This Marriage was solemnized between Us { The Mark of John Ridout / The mark of Susanna Ridout late Shore

...e of { The Mark of William Ridout / John Simonds Jun.r

Figure 19: John and Susanna's marriage, 1781

There was one Ridout couple in Sherborne who baptised their children William (22nd March 1749), Sarah (4th May 1758) and John (8th September 1753). The couple in question was Christopher Ridout and Elizabeth Parker, who married at Sherborne Abbey on Tuesday 5th May 1746. If this is the correct family, then William would have been about thirty when he married and John about twenty-eight. Obviously, Christopher is a particularly relevant first name amongst Sherborne Ridouts but, however tempting, this isn't proof that I'm on the right track, of course!

When trying to trace backwards through time, genealogists sometimes assume about thirty years between generations as a rough rule of thumb. So, if Christopher and Elizabeth were baptising children in the early 1750's I thought that Christopher may have been born about thirty years earlier, say in the early 1720s. I could only find one baptism for a Christopher Ridout anywhere in Dorset at about this time: Christopher Ridout, son of John and Mary Ridout, baptised on Thursday 2nd April 1722 at Sherborne Abbey. For a family historian, seeing 'John and Mary' is rather depressing, being probably two of the most common names in England but, after a lot of number crunching and elimination of improbable baptisms, I chose John Ridout and Mary Symonds, who married on the 1st January 1718/1719. Using my 'thirty year rule' again I guessed that John was born in about 1690 and I did find a baptism on 13th November 1691: 'John, son of John and Elizabeth Ridout'. Unfortunately, at this point, I did not know who John and Elizabeth were!

The 'other' John, born earlier, in about 1750, could perhaps have been a son of (another!) John and Mary Ridout, and was baptised in Sherborne on 21st October 1751. So, with two Johns and possibly others no definitive tree could be constructed:

John Ridout = Elizabeth?
|
John Ridout (bp.1691) = Mary Symonds
|
Christopher Ridout (bp.1722) = Elizabeth Parker
|
John Ridout (bp.1753) = Susanna Shore

or...

John Ridout (?) = Mary ?
|
John Ridout (bp.1751) = Susanna Shore

Interestingly, the Sherborne Almshouse Archive shows that a Christopher and Elizabeth Ridout were taken separately into the house as 'poor' folk on respectively 21st December 1784 (deceased by 31st August 1786) and 12th February 1787 (deceased by 31st July 1787). Unfortunately, there are no ages given for these people who may, or may not, be in the first tree above; I could find no burial records for this couple either, or at least not in Sherborne.

12. 'John Ridout IV' (c.1753-1827): man of mystery

I tend to refer to my x4 great grandfather as 'John Ridout IV' sometimes to avoid getting muddled with other men of the same name. John was probably born between 1750 and 1753; I hypothesised that he might have been the son of Christopher and Elizabeth and a brother to William and Sarah or perhaps a son of an unknown John and Mary.

Other than his marriage, his children's baptisms and what are probably his burial, my x4 great grandfather's presence in Sherborne seems to be not much recorded. He is not in the Sherborne Manor records but perhaps he did not live or work within Lord Digby's estate. He was not in early trade directories but then perhaps he either didn't have a trade or was not wealthy enough to advertise the fact. Was he a poor man? I don't think so as he doesn't appear in parish records receiving alms, nor was he the subject of settlement or removal orders. Another reason for thinking that John may not have been too badly off is because his sons had apprenticeships that the parish did not provide, as far as I know. My x3 great grandfather John (and his brother Samuel at some point in his life) was a cabinet maker; the cost of such an apprenticeship in 1800 was about £25, a considerable sum for an impoverished father to pay.

When I know nothing but vital statistics for an individual, my approach in trying to add some colour to them is to find out what I know of their family and friends in order to make some educated guesses as to the individual himself. To this end, I looked at the marriages of John's sons; his eldest boy, my x3 great grandfather John, married twice. His first wife, in 1807, was Sarah Hodges; I know little of her family but one of the witnesses at their marriage was a lady called Mary Towers. Mary's maiden name was COTTELL (aka Cottle) and she belonged to a prominent Bath family; her father George was a baker and biscuit maker who had a shop in Cross Bath Lane, near Stall Street. George's sister Jane married Charles MILSOM, son of Daniel, a schoolteacher and a member of the Bath Corporation after whom the world famous Milsom Street in Bath was named. Mary Cottell married William TOWERS in 1780 in Sherborne. In 1815, their daughter Mary married John Ridout's younger brother Charles. So clearly the families had a long and close association.

The Towers family was involved with the Sherborne Mercury, of which William was the editor. This was a hugely influential newspaper, particularly as its news coverage and distribution went well beyond that of the boundaries of Dorset. It was first published by Robert Goadby (1721-1778), a printer and bookseller. Joseph Towers, William's brother, was apprenticed to Goadby in 1753. Both families were liberal minded non-conformists.

Figure 20: Bristol Mercury banner

John Ridout's second wife was Martha Somerton, sister of the journalist and proprietor of the Bristol Mercury newspaper (Fig. 20), William Henry Somerton. Martha's brother and nephews were articulate and educated men and it seems reasonable to assume that Martha grew up under the same influences. The Somerton family as a whole may have followed no particular religious path but I John's children with Martha were baptised in the Countess of Huntingdon's Chapel in Bath, a breakaway Methodist group.

So, 'John Ridout IV' associated with at least three middle class, educated families two of which his sons married into. Is it unreasonable to think that John is likely to have been cut from similar cloth? With this thought in mind, I went to the Dorset Record Office to search for a John Ridout in Sherborne between 1753 and 1828 and I found two items worthy of note.

In 1780 and 1782, the Sherborne Land Tax records show a Mr John Ridout who owned a property in the Nethercombe parish of Sherborne, paying £1-11-0 in tax (at 4 shillings in the pound this would value his property at about £7-15-0).

In the Sherborne Militia Ballot List, record number LA/3/9/16 dated 23rd November 1798 for Westbury tithing is the entry: Jno Ridout 'served'

The 1757 Militia Act directed that militia regiments be re-established in England and Wales. Since it was unlikely that sufficient volunteers would come forward, a type of conscription was introduced by which means parishes made lists of adult males and held ballots to choose those for compulsory service. Militia Ballot Lists contained the names of all men between the ages of eighteen and forty-five eligible for the ballot.

The Westbury tithing of Sherborne included Hyle Farm, West Mill and fields and houses in the area including Acreman Street, which runs up towards Nethercombe. John Ridout must have been between 18 and 45 years to have been included in this list and clearly he had served in the militia before, which exempted him service in 1798. My x4 great grandfather, John Ridout was baptised the early 1750s – he would have been in his mid forties; could this entry relate to him? Maybe, but I also have to consider that this man may have been from a different family, for example, he could have been the brother of James Ridout (see Chapter 17); it is interesting that the two records related to the same area, Nethercombe. Obviously it seemed worth pursuing any instance of Ridouts in that area of Sherborne.

13. Nethercombe Ridouts in Sherborne: is this my family?

Apparently, there were Ridouts in Nethercombe well before the 18th century. I started my research with the Sherborne Manor survey of 1677 which revealed a new Ridout family which could be mine:

(1) 1677 Sherborne Manor Survey, homage of Nethercombe.

Manorial surveys, conducted periodically for the benefit of the Lord of the Manor, listed his tenants with the acreage of the properties that they leased and the three 'lives' upon them.

> Tenant: John Ridout of Acreman Street for 99 years if [he should live so long]
> Estates in being: He 20. Elizabeth his wife & John Parker, son of Rich'd Parker of Sutton
> Tenements: Parcell of a tenement. Late Banwells. A barne & backside
> Acres: Meadow 3½; Arable 20½; Total 29.
> Yearly rent: 14s Quarterly. Yearly value besides the rents: 10li
> Herriot: Best beast or goods

So, John Ridout, aged twenty (born ~1657) was married to Elizabeth, who may or may not have been related to the other 'life' John PARKER, son of Richard Parker of Sutton. As John was only 20, John and Elizabeth had probably not been married that long but I couldn't find any record in the Sherborne parish registers or elsewhere, recording this marriage.

(2) 1687 Roll 41 1683/4 Articles of agreement

"3 June 1687. John Ridout of Akeman Street yeoman. The Earl of Bristol agrees to let him have an Estate granted to him by lease in reversion after his own life for 99 years in Elizabeth the daughter of Richard Porter & John the son of same Richard Porter of Sutton in the County of Somerset do so long live. i.e a barn, 29 acres of ground belonging now in occupation of said John Ridout. John Ridout makes his mark it is witnessed by William Ridout who can write."

This agreement was made ten years later than the manor survey above. John Ridout of Acreman Street would now be about 30 years old and it is apparent that he is one of three lives on a lease for 29 acres of land, sharing with two children of Richard PORTER of Sutton: Elizabeth and John. The acreage is the same as that of 'Banwell's tenement' and therefore this seems to be referring to the same John Ridout and the same tenancy. Is it a coincidence that the other lives are still named as Elizabeth and John, as in 1677? This might infer that Richard Porter of Sutton and Richard Parker of Sutton are one and the same but in 1687 Elizabeth is not named as John's wife, only as Richard's daughter.

Fortunately, I found an entry for a marriage licence in the names of John Ridout of Sherborne, Dorset, yeoman, and Elizabeth Porter, of Sutton Montis, spinster, aged 23. It was interesting to see that John could not sign his name, although William Ridout could. The father apparently consented (it was not stated whose father) and the marriage was to take place at Wells St. Cuthbert on the 20th June 1687. Sutton Montis is a village in the parish of South Cadbury, Somerset, five miles south of Sherborne (Fig. 21).

Figure 21: St Cuthbert's, Wells

(3) Sherborne Estates Leases document (1709-1806)

This gives details of a fine (fee) of £21.10s imposed for changing the 'lives' on a leasehold property, dated 5th July 1710, of which Morgan LODGE was the tenant. A third life, Thomas Oliver, son of Thomas Oliver of Castletown, was added to that of Elizabeth Ridout and John Porter.

The property was described: "his estate in the tenement of late John Ridout in Acreman Street. Lodge is to have the Liberty to dig Quarr and dispose of stones in about 3 yards of the premises lying on Old Quarr, of wch stones my Lord reserves to himself the power of raising and carrying away so many as his Honour shall think fitt for his own use."

From this document it appears that by July 1710 John Ridout Jr of Acreman Street had died, leaving a widow Elizabeth. There is a burial record at Sherborne Abbey for John Ridout on 23rd August 1709. The two remaining lives on this lease were Elizabeth Ridout and John Porter, identical to those in both earlier documents. John's 'life' was to be replaced by that of Thomas Oliver.

So who was John Ridout of Acreman Street? As he had been born in about 1657, I at first assumed that he was the man who had married Elizabeth Oliver, until I found the details of his marriage to Elizabeth Porter and his death in 1709. I wonder if John Ridout and Elizabeth Porter could the x7 great grandparents for whom I have been searching i.e. the parents of the John baptised in 1691? The other entries in the 1677 survey provide more helpful information:

(4) 1677 Sherborne Manor Survey, homage of Hound Street

> Tenant: Thomas Ridout assignee of John Ridout his father decd. for 99 years if.
> Estates in being: William Ridout 17 his brother and the same Thomas 11. Cary Boucher son of Sam.
> Tenements: A rovelesse tenement with appurtenances called Swynes Well, formerly ffosters.
> Acres: pasture 1, meadow 8, arable 29. Total 33
> Yearly rent: 1li 7s ½d Quarterly. Yearly value besides the rents: 10li
> Herriott: best beast or goods.

Summarising, a man named John Ridout, who lived in Nethercombe and had died before 1677, had two possibly three sons: William in 1659/60 and Thomas in 1666 and maybe John in 1657. John Sr may have leased one or both of 'Banwell's' and 'Wyne's Well'[e] (sometimes described as 'Swyne's Well' or 'Swingwell') tenements. From available records, I believe that this is the John Ridout who left a will, written on the 15th February 1671/2 (probate 18th May 1672) in which he referred to his son John, to whom he leaves 'part of Banwell Tenement lying in Sherborne' and also says:

"Whereas my brother Thomas Ridout deceased did by his will give my son Thomas a legacy of one hundred pounds, which said legacy I used in the buying of an estate and tenement called Swingwell in Sherborne aforesaid I do therefore give and bequeath the said tenement Swingwell and the appurtenances unto my said son Thomas."

John mentioned his five children: John, William, Thomas, Mary and Elizabeth, all of whom were under the age of 21 in 1672. I found appropriately dated baptisms for these children to parents John and Alse (Alice) Ridout. In his will, John did not mention a wife but bequeathed the sum of £10 to 'Sister Elizabeth Toogood, for her care of my children' implying that he was a widower. In due course, John's son William, who wrote his will in 1682, mentioned his 'Aunt Elizabeth Toogood, spinster' and also his 'Uncle William Toogood'. This suggests that John Ridout's wife was formerly Alse or Alice Toogood. A burial record exists: 'Alice, wife of John Ridout, buried on the 17th May 1670'; John was buried as 'a widower' on the 23rd February 1671/2. Apart from naming his late brother Thomas, John also mentioned a brother William who he appointed as one of his executors. The most likely candidate for Thomas Ridout, John's elder brother, seems to be this man, who dictated his last will and testament on the 13th May 1668 and which went to probate on the 5th December of that year:

"That upon or about the thirteenth day of may in the yeare of our Lord God one thousand six hundred sixty and eight Thomas Ridout late of Leigh in the County of Dorsett being sicke of the sickness whereof he afterwards died but of perfect mynd and memory and having an intention to settle and dispose of his estate did make and declare his last will and testament ... or by word of mouth as following or to the like effect. Viz I will or I do give my wife my .... And all my goods within doores and without and one hundred pounds in money and I give her my meads at Holwell during her life and after her decease I give the meades to John Ridout during the terme of yeares or estates that I have in it. I give also one hundred pounds to John Ridouts younger sonne Thomas. I give Anne Hole, the eldest daughter of

Edward Hole twenty pounds. John Ridout shall be my executor and he shall have all the rest."

I also found the will of a lady that some researchers believe was Thomas' wife, Marjorie or Margery Ridout (misspelt 'RIDEON') née JEANES, proved in August 1669. Like Thomas, Margery mentioned no children, only siblings. She left money for the 'poor of Holwell' and was buried in Holwell churchyard whereas Thomas was buried at Sherborne Abbey on the 18th May 1668; I found it unusual for a married couple to be interred separately and so the identity of Thomas's wife is still perhaps open to question. Unfortunately, in his will Thomas did not name his wife when he left her 'meades in Holwell', a village about six miles SE of Sherborne, yet both Thomas and Margery were 'of Leigh', a village about six miles SSW from Sherborne. Arthur Ridout identified Thomas Ridout 'of Leigh' as the son of William Ridowte1 of Hyle and a brother of William Ridout[3] [as described in Chapter 3] and John Ridout, husband of Alice Toogood [Ridout book, page 9]. Whilst I believe that Thomas Ridout of Leigh and Alice's husband John were brothers, I don't think that they were sons of William[1] or brothers of William[3] [see Chapter 11 tree].

Footnote:

e. According to Joseph Fowler, in his book 'Mediaeval Sherborne' (p.230), 'Wynneswell' may have been a corruption of St Winifred's Well, an old spring in Ottery Lane in the Westbury tithing of Sherborne.

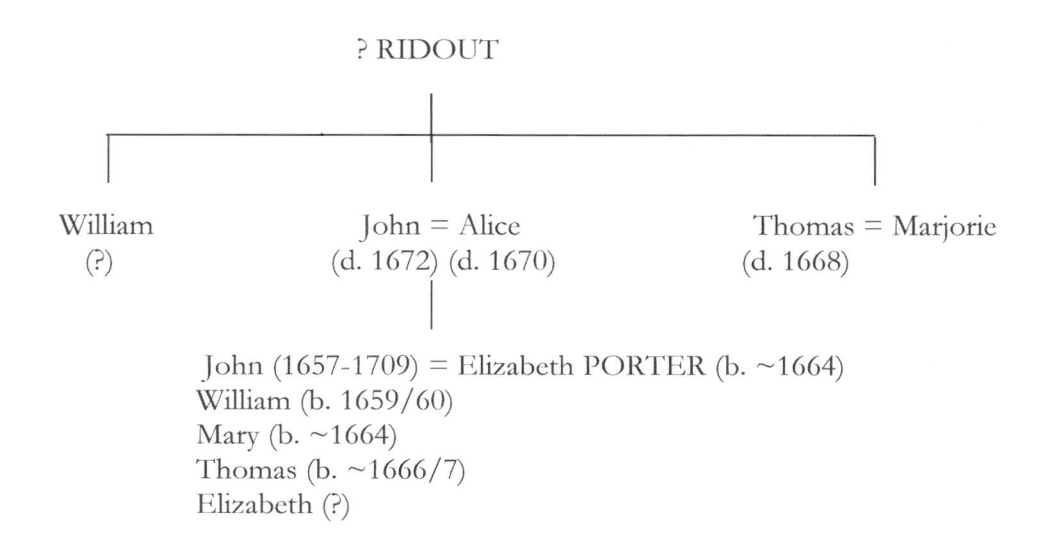

? RIDOUT

William (?)

John = Alice
(d. 1672) (d. 1670)

Thomas = Marjorie
(d. 1668)

John (1657-1709) = Elizabeth PORTER (b. ~1664)
William (b. 1659/60)
Mary (b. ~1664)
Thomas (b. ~1666/7)
Elizabeth (?)

14. London Ridouts: yellow shoes and blue murder!

John Ridout and Elizabeth Porter married in 1687. Amongst others, they had sons John (b. 1691)[f] and Porter (b. 1699/1700). Porter married a woman called Abigail whose surname, I believe, was HIBDITCH. A female of this name was baptised in Sherborne, daughter of James and Jane, on the 21st February 1698/9 and the reasons that I believe this to be Porter's wife are threefold. Firstly, the couple had several children (John bp. 28th July 1731; Porter bp. 25th April, 1733, James bp. 10th September 1735, Mary bp. 4th January 1738/9, Thomas bp. 11th August 1744 and Anne bp. 14th January 1747/8) of which 'Roger Hibditch Ridout' (bp. 30th July 1740) was the only child to be given a middle name; it was not uncommon for this to reflect the mother's maiden name. Secondly, in the will of Bernard Hibditch (1734) the testator says that he is father-in-law of Richard Porter, a relative of John's wife Elizabeth. Thirdly, Porter Ridout Jr mentioned his 'kinswoman Ann Hibditch' in his will and she is known to have lived with him as his servant at a later time.

Figure 22: Company of Cordwainers

Porter and Abigail's son Porter left Sherborne at some point and went to London. He purchased a Freedom of the City of London on Thursday 5th June 1760, paying 46 shillings and 8 pence, which helped to 'discharge the debt of the City.' Porter Jr joined the Livery Company of Cordwainers (Fig. 22) where he was said to be 'son of Porter of Sherborne, farmer.' On the 19th April 1761, he married Elizabeth HUGHES, a widow from Duke's Place, Aldgate; Porter was from St Katharine Cree, a parish nearby. The couple married at St James's Church in the bride's parish and the next year Elizabeth had a son Jeremiah who was baptised at Duke's Place on the 11th June 1762. Perhaps as a consequence of the birth, Elizabeth died a few weeks later; there is an administration of her estate to Porter dated 28th September 1762. Having found a will for Elizabeth's first husband Thomas Hughes (prob. 1759), a distiller and coffeeman of Duke's Place, it seems probable that this is how Porter came to Aldgate, took over 'Tom's Coffee House' and stayed there for the next two decades.

Porter married a second time to Elizabeth MORRIS, a young spinster from Barking in Essex. An allegation was made and signed at St James's on the 26th November 1764 and the couple married a year later, on the 17th November 1765 at St James's, Duke's Place. I have found no children of this marriage.

From 1763 to 1784, Porter is shown in Land Tax records for London, paying variable amounts in tax for his property at Duke's Place, usually about £2 12s 0d. An entry for 1784 gave his address more specifically as 'Broad Court'. Comparing tax entries across these years, it seems that Porter had stayed at this same address throughout his time in the area. Perhaps his life was for the most part straightforward and untroubled but one night things were to change very drastically.

On the 20th October, 1784, Porter Ridout was indicted:

"that he, not having the fear of God before his eyes, but being moved and seduced by the instigation of the Devil, on the 7th of October, in the 24th year of his Majesty's reign with force and arms, at London, in the parish of St. James's, Duke's-place, upon Moses Lazarus, in the peace of God and our Lord the King then and there being, did make an assault, and with a certain gun, value 1 shilling, then and there loaded with gun-powder and leaden shot, which he held in both his hands, to, at and against the said Moses, feloniously, wilfully, and of his malice aforethought, did shoot and discharge, and him the said Moses in and upon the right breast, and in and upon the right side of the body, near the upper part of the belly, did then and there feloniously, wilfully, and of his malice aforethought, strike and wound giving to him the said Moses in and upon the said right side of the breast, one mortal wound of the depth of four inches and of the width of one half quarter of an inch, and in and upon the right side of the body near the upper part of the belly, another mortal wound of the depth of three inches and of the width of one half quarter of an inch, of which he instantly died: and the Jurors say that the said Porter Ridout, him the said Moses Lazarus did kill and murder. He was likewise charged on the coroner's inquisition with the like murder." Old Bailey Proceedings Online (www.oldbaileyonline.org) October 1784.

Porter's coffee house was in the Jewish quarter; the Synagogue was not far away. On this day in October, the locals were celebrating the Simchat Torah, marking the conclusion of the Feast of the Tabernacles; the men and boys were always rather rowdy during this festival and Duke's Place (Fig. 23) was very crowded. Apparently, Porter had attempted to remonstrate with some men who were throwing squibs and fire crackers at his house. In so doing he was set upon by the crowd, had his pocket picked and sustained several minor injuries. Managing to break away, he fled to his house hotly pursued by the angry mob. He and his servant, Ann Hibditch, managed between them to close the door against the rioters and Porter was seen moments later, standing at an open upstairs window holding a gun which he fired randomly into the crowd below. The shot comprised some small lead pellets normally used to scour the insides of glass bottles but, unfortunately, they penetrated the flesh of a thirteen year old boy who subsequently died.

Figure 23: The Great Synagogue, Duke's Place, ~1820

Defended by Mr William Garrow, a very eminent barrister of the day and after many character witnesses had spoken in his favour, Porter was found innocent of wilful murder and set free. The full transcript of the case can be seen at the 'Old Bailey Proceedings' online. Anti-Semitism was never suggested as a motive for this killing; on the contrary, Porter seemed to have many friends in the neighbourhood, some of whom gave evidence of his good character. He had also worked as a Peace Officer in the community and could speak Hebrew.

However, the last tax record for Porter in Duke's Place in 1784 indicates that, not surprisingly, he could no longer stay in the area and so moved away. He died and was buried at Bunhill Fields, a non-conformist cemetery in London on the 4th April 1793. His will, dated 2nd March 1793 and proved the 8th April, shows that, now a self styled 'gentleman', Porter had been living in the quiet suburb of Camberwell in Surrey. He bequeathed £2,000 to Ann Hibditch, his kinswoman along with many household goods. He also gave money to his married sister Ann (surname illegible) and left the residue of his estate to 'my loving son Jeremiah'.

Jeremiah Ridout, born in ~1762 at Duke's Place was still a young man when his father died. On the 25th September 1788, he married Martha MEDLEY at St Andrew's by the Wardrobe, her parish, whilst his was said to be 'St Magdalen & St Gregory'. Clearly he had not stayed at Duke's Place either. A description states: '…the church of St Mary Magdalene Old Fish Street with St Gregory by St Paul is situated on the north side of Knightrider Street at the west corner of the Old Change' (very close to St Paul's Cathedral). Jeremiah was listed in the London Poll Book 1796, under the Liverymen, in the Company of Cordwainers, as 'Jeremiah Ridout, cordwainer of Little Knight Rider Street.' I have not found any children of this marriage and presumably Martha died as, on the 22nd December 1794, Jeremiah married a second time to Sarah SMITH. The wedding took place at the bride's parish in Stoke Newington; she was a spinster and he was 'a widower of St Mary Magdalen, Fish Street'.

Jeremiah and Sarah had two daughters, Sarah, bp. 26th July 1800 at St Clement Dane's Church, Westminster and Mary bp. 22nd May 1802 at St Stephen's Church, Exeter. Clearly, the family moved around quite a bit! Both of these baptisms were recorded retrospectively at Dr. William's Library of Nonconformist Registers. Helpfully, a record of the bride's birth in 1762 added her parent's names as Reuben and Sarah Smith. Reuben was a soap boiler and shopkeeper from Bilderstone, Hadleigh in Suffolk; his family were 'Independents.'

> Beneath this stone
> are deposited the remains of
> **SARAH**
> *wife of Jeremiah Ridout*
> who died December 13th 1830
> Aged 64 years
>
> ALSO OF
> **JEREMIAH RIDOUT**
> who died Feb 15th 1842
> Aged 79 years
>
> Low Tomb.
>
> The late William Wills, Esq., Solicitor, of Birmingham, married a daughter of Jeremiah and Sarah Ridout.

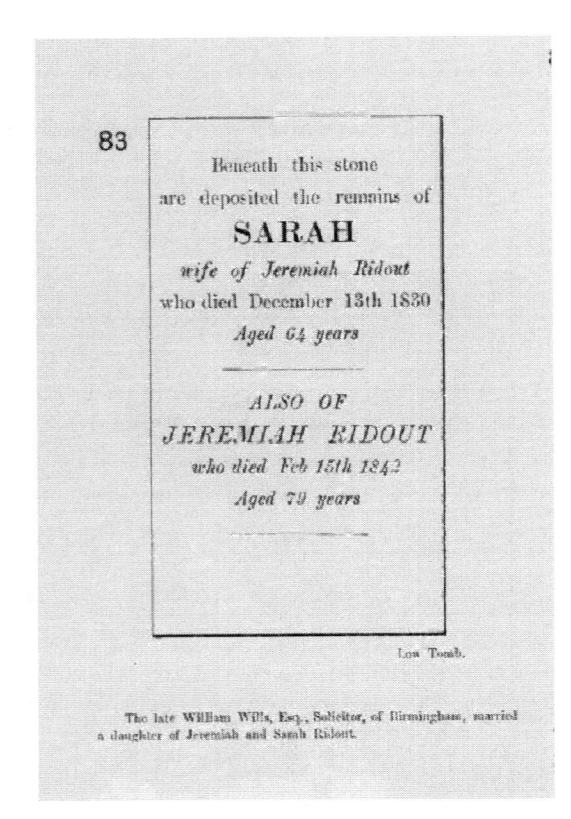

Figure 24: Tomb inscription

Jeremiah moved to Birmingham at some point; local newspapers showed the sale of many properties belonging to him in the Hagley-Row (Hagley Road) area of Edgbaston, the marriage of Jeremiah's daughters and then the death of his wife Sarah in 1830 (Coventry Herald, 24th Dec) aged sixty-four years; all in the same area. Jeremiah's death was reported in the Coventry Herald on the 25th February 1842: "In his 81st year, Jeremiah Ridout Esq. of Edgbaston who for many years carried on a business as an American merchant." (Fig. 24). Sarah married William WILLS and Mary married Henry William Gardner WREFORD.

It is not clear just what goods Jeremiah the merchant sold; a fire insurance policy for the Sun Company, dated 31st July 1811 was taken out for 'Messrs Ridout and co, Knight Rider Street, merchant' and looking again at insurance records, I found that the earliest one was dated 1785 for Porter Ridout's premises at No. 9 Knight Rider Street. So, the business had been running for nearly thirty years but I can find no references or advertisements of relevance.

One interesting thing about this investigation so far is that 'present at the birth' of Sarah Ridout in Norfolk Street in 1800 was a 'J G Ridout'. The only Ridout man that I know from my records with these initials was Dr John Gibbs Ridout (1575-1823) who lived near Blackfriars Bridge, quite close to Knight Rider Street; he was the son of George Ridout (1701-1779) and grandson of Christopher (1669-1743). Does this imply that the Nethercombe Ridouts belong to this part of the Sherborne tree? Not necessarily; Dr Ridout was trained in midwifery and may well have attended the birth quite by coincidence (Fig. 25).

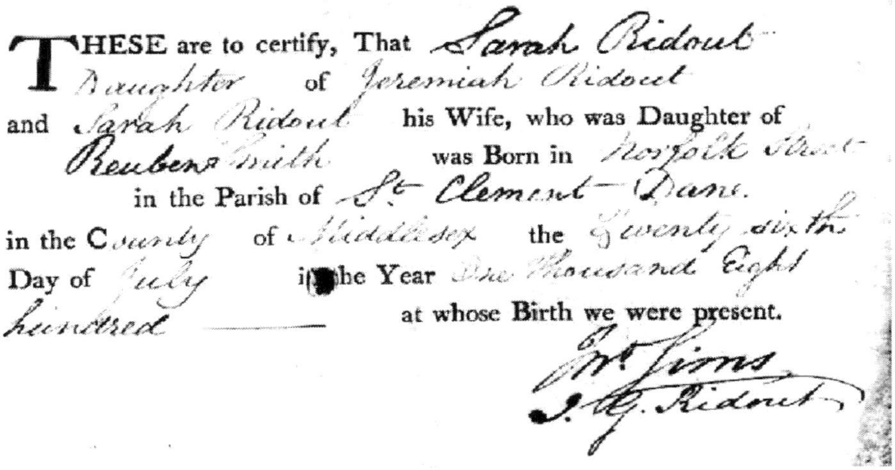

THESE are to certify, That Sarah Ridout Daughter of Jeremiah Ridout and Sarah Ridout his Wife, who was Daughter of Reuben Smith was Born in Norfolk Street in the Parish of St Clement Danes in the County of Middlesex the Twenty sixth Day of July in the Year One Thousand Eight hundred ——— at whose Birth we were present.

W. Sims

J. G. Ridout

Figure 25: Dr John Gibbs Ridout attends Sarah's birth

Even after leaving London for Birmingham, Jeremiah retained his right to vote in the City of London; the 1838 Poll Book for the Parish of St Lawrence Cheapside and others show that he qualified by having a freehold property at 27 King Street, a thoroughfare that runs from Cheapside to the church of St Lawrence Jewry.

Knowing that Jeremiah Ridout had died in 1842, I looked for his will, which I found dated 3rd March 1841. It ran for several pages and mentioned his daughters, their husbands and children. There were no helpful references to other Ridouts but Jeremiah did mention his freehold properties in Knight Rider Street, Duke's Place and Edgbaston. I noticed that there was another will listed under 'Jeremiah Ridout' dated 14th July 1786 and so, out of curiosity, I read it. The contents were very interesting but rather confusing!

"I Jeremiah Ridout, Citizen and Cordwainer of London do make my last Will and Testament in manner following Videlecit I desire my Body may be interred at the discretion of my Executor herein after named in my family vault in Bunhill ffields Burial Ground and as touching other Worldly Estate wherewith it has pleased God to bless me I dispose of the same

as follows and first I give and devise all and every my ffreehold Messuages Tenements and Hereditaments situate in King Street Poor Jewry Lane and Duke's Place London and all other my real Estates whatsoever and wheresoever unto Edward Jefferies of Lothbury London Blackwell hall factor and his heirs To the use Use Intent and purpose that Mary How my servant in case she shall be living at the time of my decease….."

The annuity was to be paid from the rents of his various properties and, after a number of other bequests to Grace, widow of cousin Thomas Cray (deceased), Edward Jefferies, Stephen Lowdell, William Patful and his wife Rebecca, cousin Ann Cray, Elizabeth Southward, daughter of cousin Richard Cray (deceased) and sons of Robert Plimpton (deceased) his brother-in-law, the remainder of his properties were to be given….

"….. to the use of my Cousin Porter Ridout of Knight Rider Street London Gentleman and his assigns during the term of his natural life. He the said Porter Ridout and his assigns keeping the said ffreehold premises during such time in Tenantable repair and from and immediately after his decease subject and chargeable as aforesaid To the use of Jeremiah Ridout son of the said Porter Ridout his Heirs and assigns for ever…."

Porter received a great many personal items from his 'cousin' too, for example a gold watch, walking cane, tobacco pouch, framed prints of King William and Queen Mary, Bible, a tea service and others; these were to be passed on to his son Jeremiah after his death.

So, who was Jeremiah Ridout that died in 1787? He was buried 'in the family vault' at Bunhill Fields', as was Porter. Jeremiah had called him 'cousin'. If this was to be taken literally then it would imply that Jeremiah's father was a nephew of Porter's father, John Ridout. I set out to find this man in the available online records but, unfortunately, without knowing his age at death, this was not easy. Since Robert Plimpton was said to be Jeremiah's brother-in-law, I was not surprised to find the marriage of Jeremiah to Mary Plimpton, a spinster and daughter of Robert and Mary. The ceremony took place at All Hallow's Church in Tottenham on the 19th May 1737. The groom was from the parish of St Bartholomew the Great (West Smithfield) and the bride was from Christchurch (Middlesex). There was also an entry in the 1750 Poll Book for London which listed members of the Liveried Companies and under 'Cordwainers' was 'Jeremiah Ridout, woollen draper, Cloth-fair.' Jeremiah had mentioned this messuage later in his will which confirms that he is the right man.

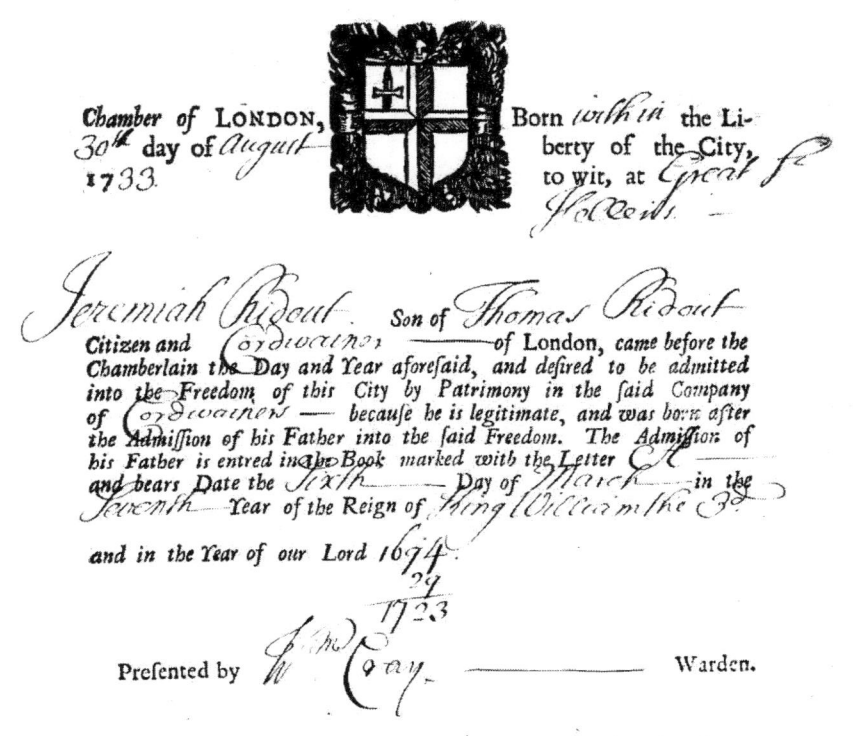

Figure 26: Jeremiah Ridout, 1733. COL/CHD/FR/02/0541-0546 (LMA)

Jeremiah was granted Freedom of the City of London on the 30th August 1733 (Fig. 26) through patrimony. This meant that the son of a Citizen could be admitted into the Freedom too, as long as he was legitimately born when his father was already a Citizen; Thomas, was made a Freeman on the 6th March 1694/5. Since Freedom was not usually granted until the applicant was at least twenty-one, Jeremiah must have been born between 1695 and 1712. I questioned the London Metropolitan Archives regarding the possible relevance of the sum shown on the document i.e. 1694 + 29 =1723 but the archivist couldn't help).

Jeremiah served an apprenticeship with William Johnson, a draper of St Bartholomew's, the duty for which was paid by Mr Johnson in 1720. Apprenticeships usually began when a boy was about fourteen, but the tax may have been paid at any point during the apprenticeship, or even afterwards, and so this does not necessarily narrow down the apprentice's birth year.

Jeremiah appeared in numerous Land Tax, Directory and Poll Books, invariably as a woollen draper of 22 Cloth Fair (Fig. 27), an aptly named street where in medieval times, merchants would trade cloth during the fair of St Bartholomew's. Great St Bart's Church is close by and the whole area is now in the London Borough of Farringdon Within, not far from Smithfield market. The Land Tax entries for Jeremiah run from 1734 to 1786, the year that he died; he seemed to have lived in the same area throughout his life. He left a will and he was buried in Bunhill Fields: 'Mr Jeremiah Ridout, Cloth Faire, buried 5th December 1786; in a vault, 14s' (RG4/3986/127).

I found the will of Thomas, Ridout, Jeremiah's father, dated 26th October 1732 (probate granted 8th June 1734) which, after the customary salutations, continues ...

"In the Name of God Amen. I Thomas Ridout Citizen and Cordwainer ... whereas I have in my life advanced and paid unto my loving son Jeremiah Ridout the sum of one thousand pounds of lawfull money of Great Britain in setting him up in the Trade and business of a Woollen Draper which he now useth, therefore I do by this my will bequeath unto my said son Jeremiah Ridout only the sum of ffive pounds of like money for Mourning. I give and bequeath unto my son Thomas Ridout and unto my daughter Ann ffox the wife of james ffox and my son John Ridout and to each of them ffive pounds apiece of like money for Mourning. Item I give and bequeath unto Jeremiah Cray of Bishop Stoffod in the county of

Figure 27: Rear of 22 Cloth Fair, c. 1904

Hertford Upholsterer twenty pounds of like money. I give and bequeath unto my son in law William Cray Citizen and Cordwainer the like sum of twenty pounds of like money. All the rest residue and remainder of my money stock in Trade goods chattels and personall Estate whatsoever and wheresoever (my debts and Legacies herein before given being first paid and satisfied) I will shall be divided into three equal parts or shares and third part whereof I give and bequeath unto my loving son the said Thomas Ridout and other Third part or share I give and bequeath unto my daughter the said Ann now wife of James ffox to be paid her within twelve months next after my decease by my executor herein after named and the other remaining third part or share thereof I give and bequeath unto my said loving son John Ridout to be paid him by my executor herein after named att his age of twenty and one years."

Thomas listed various freehold properties he had in London: including King Street, St Lawrence Lane, the Crown Coffee House, Poor Jury Lane and Dukes Place which he gives to Thomas with provisos to share the rental proceeds with his siblings such that they were treated equally. The London Magazine (vol. 3 p. 328; 1734) reported his death on the 3rd June as: 'Mr Thomas Ridout, shoe-maker, near Aldgate, reputed to be worth 10,000L [£].' Thomas also mentioned in his will Mr William Cray, Citizen and Cordwainer and Mr Thomas Cray, Citizen and Apothecary, sons-in-law.

So, Thomas Ridout appears to have at least four children alive at the time he made his will in 1732: Jeremiah, Thomas, Anne and John, but he made no mention of a wife and therefore it is probable that she had pre-deceased him. Thomas (a bachelor) had married Mary CRAY (a spinster) on the 14th April 1695 at St James's, Duke's Place; she was the daughter of Richard Cray. I found Thomas's burial in Bunhill Fields: 'Mr Ridout, Allgate, buried 6th June 1734; in a single grave, cost 13s 6d' (ref: RG4/3978/102).

Having been unable to find baptisms for Thomas and Mary's children (possibly due to non-conformism) it was only possible, using logic, to calculate a rough idea of likely birth years.

A document, dated 1728 showed that Thomas Ridout, son of Thomas Ridout, cordwainer, had qualified for Freedom by virtue of having signed on as an apprentice with his father for a term of seven years from the 7th May 1712. If Thomas had been fourteen when he began his apprenticeship, and had to be at least twenty-one in 1728, he must have been born between 1698 and 1706.

Thomas Jr was listed as a shoemaker in Shoemaker Row in 1750 as was another shoemaker, James DAVIS. The men formed a very successful business partnership and I was surprised to see photographs of some of their ladies ladies shoes online (Fig. 28); amazing to think that some pairs have survived nearly three centuries! Interestingly, Shoemaker Row was renamed Duke Street and later, Duke's Place, the same street on which Porter Ridout lived a few years later. Thomas died in 1768 and left a will; I also found his burial in Bunhill Fields: 'Mr Thomas Ridout from Shoreditch, buried 10th October 1768; in a vault, cost 14s 0d' (ref: RG4/4633/91).

Figure 28: Thomas Ridout shoes © The Metropolitan Museum of Art

Thomas senior's son John was under the age of twenty-one when Thomas made his will in 1732, therefore he could not have been born earlier than 1711. I found John's Freedom of the City of London papers; he was accepted during early April 1737, indicating that his approximate birth year was ~1716. John died in 1741, a young man; he left a will and was buried in Bunhill Fields: 'Mr Ridout from Bishopsgate buried on 30th November 1741; in a vault, cost 14s 0d' (ref: RG4/3980/22).

In contrast, by 1732 Thomas and Mary's daughter Anne was married, to James Fox; their wedding was on the 19th August 1728 at St Saviour's Church in Denmark Park, Southwark. Unfortunately, the parish records gave no details other than names and so this reveals nothing of the bride's age but, supposing at the youngest she was eighteen, Anne would have been born in ~1710 or before. As there was more than one entry for Anne or James Fox amongst the non-conformist burials at Bunhill, I cannot identify the years of either of their deaths.

How this family and that of John Ridout and Elizabeth are connected was not clear at first. Thomas Ridout (d. 1734) made no mention of Porter Ridout in his will but his son, Jeremiah called Porter 'cousin' and mentioned Porter's son Jeremiah as well. Looking at all the ages and dates, it would be virtually impossible for Thomas's son Jeremiah and Porter Ridout to actually be first cousins, but it was common practice in the 17th and 18th centuries for 'cousin' to sometimes mean 'nephew' or 'niece', according to many genealogical references. Given the level of property, both real and personal, that Jeremiah gave to Porter and his son, one might infer that the relationship was fairly close. Oddly, just as I was reaching the end of this piece of research, I unexpectedly came across a page in Boyd's 'Inhabitants of London and Boyd's Family Units' found on an online genealogical pay site. This record, made by Percival Boyd (1866-1955), a prodigious indexer, suggests that Thomas Ridout, the father of Jeremiah ('Jeremy'), Thomas and John by Mary Cray had first married Susan PRITCHARD on the 7th September 1686 in St James's Duke's Place. I had seen this marriage in the parish register previously and wondered briefly whether this was the same Thomas but I dismissed the idea because in the Cray marriage Thomas was recorded as a bachelor. Now, I think what is more likely is that Thomas did marry Susanna in 1686 and fathered three female children Sarah, Edith and Elizabeth, all baptised in St Clement's Church, Eastcheap. Perhaps they and their mother died and Thomas started a new life nine years later when he married Mary. His marital status could have been a genuine oversight by the recording clerk, a lie on Thomas's behalf, or maybe even bigamy if Susan had not died! If Thomas had married as a young man, say about 20 years of age then this could easily be Thomas Ridout, baptised on the 22nd January 1665/66, son of John and Alice, brother to John Ridout (husband of Elizabeth Porter) which would mean that Thomas's son Jeremiah was a first cousin once removed of Porter Jr.

A few days after writing this chapter I had a breakthrough. As I wrote in the previous paragraph, I had the feeling that Thomas Ridout the cordwainer, father of Jeremiah, was a son of John Ridout and his wife Alice but I had no proof. I wondered by what means Thomas had gained his Freedom of the City of London but I could find no entry for him in the index to the Freedom Admission papers. I looked at each record image in turn and, after a few hours,

I was rewarded by seeing Thomas' apprenticeship indenture (Fig. 29); he started a seven year term with his master, Joseph PARSONS, Citizen and

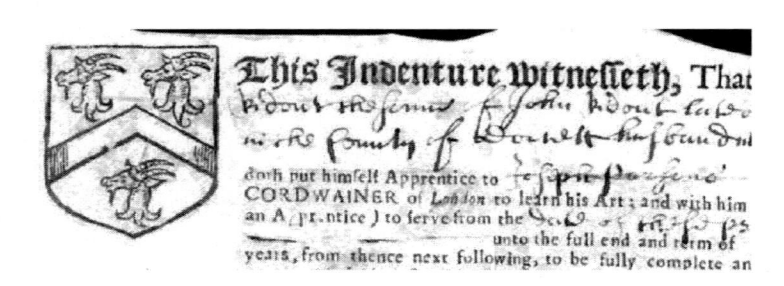

Figure 29: Thomas Ridout, 1682. COL/CHD/FR/02 (LMA)

Cordwainer on the 23rd November 1682. Better still was how Thomas was described: 'the Sonne of John Ridout, late of Sherbourne in the County of Dorsett, husbandman, deceased'. So this man was indeed who I had thought he was! A sweet moment indeed.

If Thomas had started an apprenticeship in 1682 at the usual age of about 14, his birth year would be ~1668 and he would have been just 19 on his marriage to Susanna in 1686. If Thomas had gained his Freedom when he was first able to, at 21, this would have been in 1689 (not 1695). So, it is possible that Thomas waited for six years until applying for his Freedom after finishing his apprenticeship. Why? A possibility is that, as Thomas and Susanna's first child was born on the 30th October, less than two months after their wedding; the marriage had taken place, during Thomas' apprenticeship, perhaps to legitimise their daughter. Thomas may have finished his indentures but worked at more casual labour to earn money and keep his family before finally applying for his Freedom, allowing him to develop his shoemaking business after Susanna had died; perhaps he received some financial assistance from his in-laws, the Cray family.

Footnote:

f. In Chapter 11, I traced my line back to John, son of John and Elizabeth Ridout, baptised in 1691 in Sherborne. I can now identify John Ridout and Elizabeth Porter as being this couple. However, after studying this family further, I wonder if my line may instead lead from the grandson of Porter Ridout and his wife Abigail. This couple baptised a son John on the 28th July 1731; he could have married and had a son John in the correct time frame and, indeed, there is a baptism of John Ridout, son of John and Mary on the 21st October 1751 in Sherborne. I know that 'John, son of Porter Ridout of Sherborne' was alive in 1746 as he undertook a blacksmith's apprenticeship with Matthew KING. He is also mentioned in the 1786 will of his first cousin once removed, Jeremiah Ridout of London; Jeremiah forgives John all debts with him. Finding living relatives of Porter and Abigail would be helpful in this respect since DNA testing might indicate whether or not I was on the right track. If I expanded the entire Sherborne tree to its fullest extent, I could find several candidates for the parents of my x4 great grandfather but it's unlikely I will identify him with certainty unless new evidence comes to light.

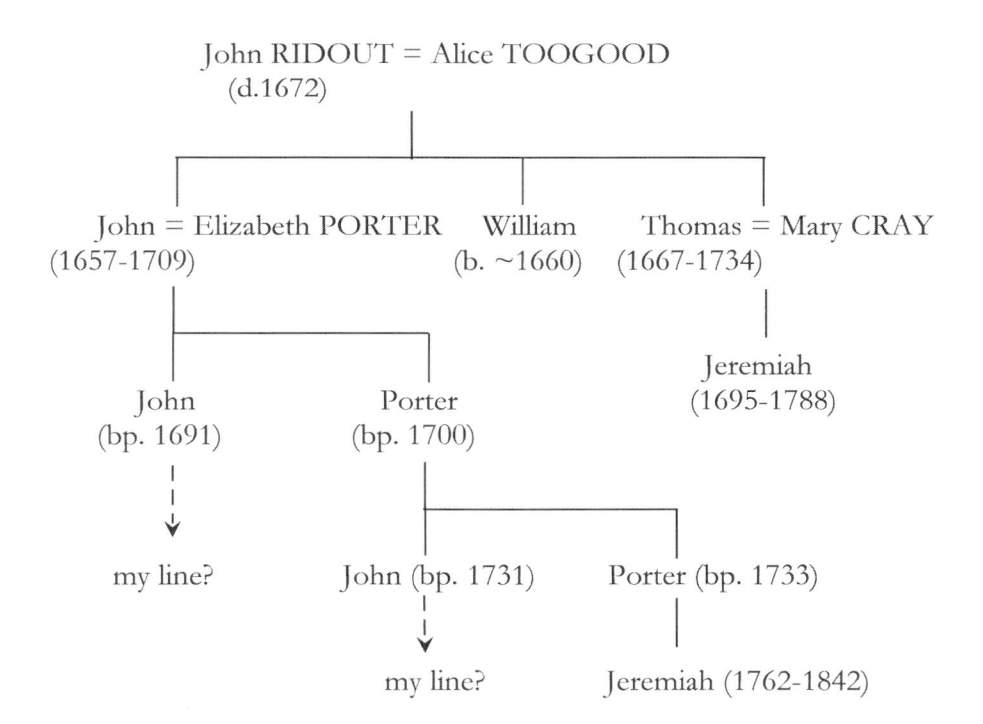

```
                John RIDOUT = Alice TOOGOOD
                    (d.1672)
        ┌───────────────┼───────────────┐
John = Elizabeth PORTER  William    Thomas = Mary CRAY
(1657-1709)            (b. ~1660)   (1667-1734)
   ┌─────────┴─────────┐                │
  John              Porter          Jeremiah
(bp. 1691)        (bp. 1700)       (1695-1788)
   ┊              ┌────┴────┐
   ▼           John (bp. 1731)   Porter (bp. 1733)
my line?          ┊                  │
                  ▼              Jeremiah (1762-1842)
              my line?
```

67

15. Elizabeth ?Oliver & Alice Toogood

I have written previously about two John Ridouts – one married Elizabeth ?Oliver and has descendants who live in Canada and the USA. The other John Ridout married Alice Toogood; their descendants went to London or stayed in Sherborne. Trying to sort out which John goes where in the entire family tree is confusing. In this chapter I will do my best to explain the logic behind my particular interpretation but, as always, this is open to challenge.

John Ridout – husband of Elizabeth ?Oliver

In the 1677 Manor Survey of Sherborne, in the homage of Nethercombe, there was a leaseholder called John Ridout of Combe (short for Nethercombe), said to be 45 years old and therefore born in about 1632; after a lot of thought I concluded that it is likely this man was John Ridout, widower of Elizabeth (? née Oliver).

In John Ridout of Combe's will (1678) he mentioned his brother-in-law Christopher Oliver (see p. 22). If John's sister Edith was Christopher Oliver's wife (mar. Sherborne on the 24th October 1654) this would mean that John's parents had a daughter Edith. Of course, the absence of a baptism is not evidence that such a child was not born, but the only Ridout couple that I know who baptised a John and an Edith were William Ridout and Julyan Toogood (John bp. 4th May 1634 and Edith bp. 3rd July 1631). Both children were mentioned by name in the will of their aunt, Magdalen Toogood, dated 1638.

Going back to the 1677 survey – in Hound Street, Sherborne the lives on a copyhold tenement described as 'formerly Rawleigh's' (previously belonging to Sir Walter Raleigh) were William Ridout Sr., 78 years and his sons Thomas Ridout., 54 years and William Ridout, 53 years. These men were, I believe, William (husband of Julyan Toogood; bp. 28th November 1599 - referred to in Chapter 8 as William²) and his sons Thomas (bp. 16th January 1623/4) and William (bp. 28th January 1625/6). If I am right, John of Combe (b. ~1632) was the brother of this Thomas and William. When genealogist Arthur Ridout constructed this family tree [Ridout book, page 9], he maintained that John of

Combe's brother Thomas had died in 1668 and left property in Holwell, giving £100 to his nephew, John's son Thomas. I believe that this is wrong as I have shown that the Thomas who died in 1668 was brother of John Ridout, husband of Alice, née Toogood (in his 1671 will, John referred to his brother Thomas's bequest and had said that the £100 had been used to buy a lease on Swingwell tenement, which he later handed over to his son; see Chapter 13).

John Ridout – husband of Alice Toogood

I don't know when this John was born but, after searching all available Dorset parish records, I think I have found a possible baptism for his wife Alse (Alice) Toogood, which took place in Sherborne Abbey on the 2nd October 1630, daughter of Robert Toogood. John (in his 1671 will) mentioned Robert Toogood and also referred to his 'brother' William Toogood, probably meaning his late wife Alice's brother. The following Abbey baptisms may be of this family…

- 23rd February 1621: Rob't, son of Rob't
- 16th June 1622: Katherine, daughter of Rob't
- 31st August 1625: Elizabeth, daughter of Rob't
- 25th April: Grace, daughter of Robti
- 8th October 1626: William, son of Robti
- 2nd October 1630: Alse, daughter of Robert
- 21st September 1634: Mary, daughter of Robert & Elizabeth
- 26th August 1635: Thomas, son of Robert

A Court of Bequests case (Dorchester Popes M.S.S Court of Bequests Chas. I Bundle 42), dated 1636, involved depositions taken from members of these Ridout and Toogood families. Here it was written that a witness, Robert Toogood's wife Elizabeth (see the baptism of Mary above), was aged forty years and that Robert was a forty-five year old husbandman. Possibly the same Robert Toogood 'of Combe', in a very brief will dated 1658, mentioned his wife, a son William and unmarried daughters Grace and Mary. Neither Alice nor Elizabeth was named but perhaps they were married, or soon to be married – if this is the correct Robert Toogood. If the Alice that was baptised in 1630 was John's wife, and making a possibly incorrect assumption that John might have been the same age or slightly older, it may be that this John was born in the decade 1620-1630. The full Ridout tree includes four married couples that baptised a son John in the appropriate time frame:

1. 25th April 1622: son of Thomas Ridout (bp. 1574) & Edith Palmer
2. 10th June 1625: son of William Ridout (bp. 1577) & Edith Oldice
3. 24th February 1630/31: son of Thomas Ridout (bp. 1601) & Eleanor
4. 4th May 1634: son of William Ridout Jr (bp. 1599) & Julyan Toogood

Assuming that William and Julyan were the parents of John who married Elizabeth ?Oliver, Alice Toogood's husband John could have been the son of either couple 1, 2 or 3. Arthur Ridout wrote that Alice's husband John was the son of couple 2, William Ridout and Edith Oldice, although he gave no reason for this [Ridout book, page 9]. Was he correct? The answer, in my opinion, is 'no' because in his 1671 will, John mentions a living brother, William, but William and Edith's son William, husband of Ann Toogood, died in 1630. His widow Ann remarried Robert Parfitt, a fact confirmed by the Court of Bequests case, mentioned above, and by the 1638 will of Magdalen Toogood in which she describes William and Ann's son William as "William Ridout the now sonne in law of Robert Parfitt of Sherborne". In the context of seventeenth century wills, 'son-in-law' often meant 'stepson'.

The elimination of two Ridout couples leaves just two sets of potential parents for Alice's John: couple 2, Thomas and Edith, or Thomas and Edith's son, Thomas and Eleanor, couple 3. If John was the son of Thomas and Edith, then his brother Thomas, who supposedly died childless in 1668, would instead be the Thomas in couple 3, who was married to Eleanor, was alive in 1672 and was far from childless! So the only couple left is Thomas and Eleanor themselves, for whom I have not found a son William baptised. Arthur Ridout thought that the John baptised in 1632 to couple 3 was the man that married Elizabeth ?Oliver [Ridout book, page 63] but I think that he was the John who married Alice Toogood; Arthur also thought that Alice's husband John had been the grandson of William of Hyle (1577-1639) [Ridout book, page 9] but I have shown that this is not possible. Perhaps in time more evidence will come along to put this tree together with certainty but for now I will stay with my hypothesis and 'switch' the couples around.

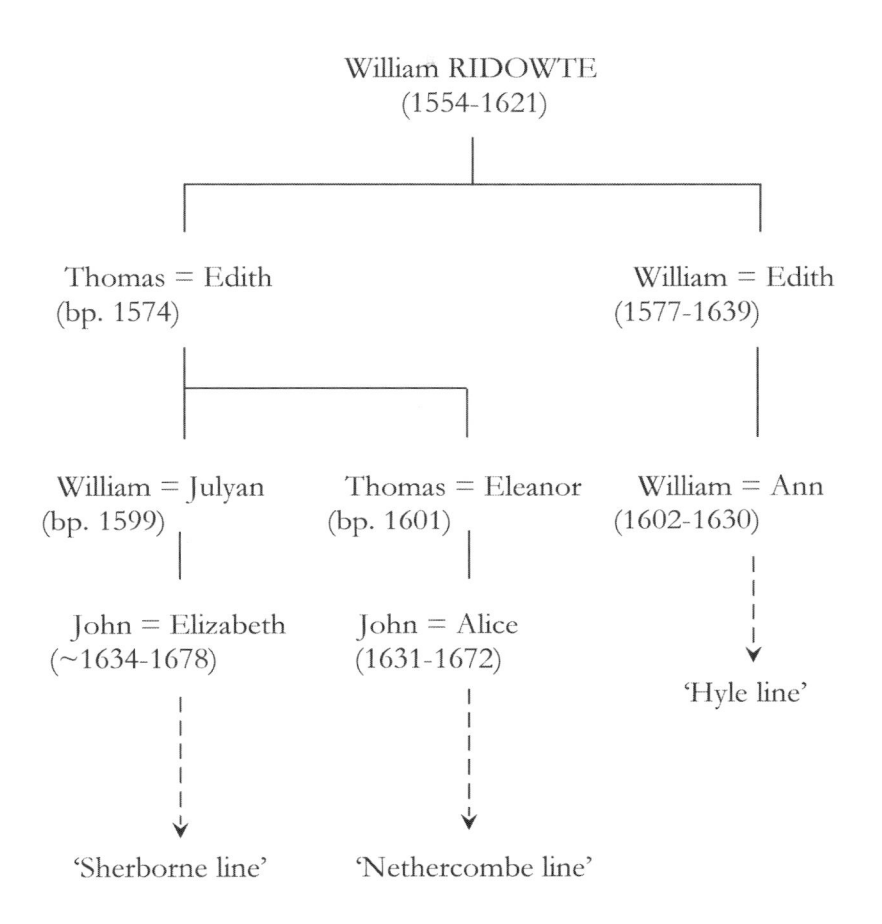

```
                    William RIDOWTE
                      (1554-1621)
                           |
         ┌─────────────────┴─────────────────┐
    Thomas = Edith                      William = Edith
    (bp. 1574)                          (1577-1639)
         |                                   |
   ┌─────┴─────┐                             |
William = Julyan   Thomas = Eleanor     William = Ann
(bp. 1599)         (bp. 1601)           (1602-1630)
    |                  |                     ¦
John = Elizabeth   John = Alice              ¦
(~1634-1678)       (1631-1672)               ↓
    ¦                  ¦                 'Hyle line'
    ¦                  ¦
    ↓                  ↓
'Sherborne line'   'Nethercombe line'
```

16. The Oliver family of Sherborne

I hypothesised that John Ridout, husband of Elizabeth ?Oliver was the son of William Ridout and his wife Julyan (née Toogood). I decided to find out more about the Oliver family of Sherborne and see if I could build on this hypothesis. Unfortunately, tracking down parish records and wills is probably the best way but the results can make for some dull reading!

The research starts with Christopher Oliver marrying Edith Ridout, possibly John's sister, on the 24th October 1654; theirs was the last marriage shown in St Mary's parish register for several decades as presumably further Sherborne marriages were written in a separate book which has since been lost. Anyway, Christopher and Edith baptised several children in Sherborne:

- 26th November 1664: Christopher, son of Christoph. and Edeth
- 17th June 1666: Marie, daughter of Christaner and Edeth
- 30th September 1667: Joane, daughter of Christopher
- 28th October 1670: Cathrin, daughter of Christopher and Edeth
- 23rd October 1672: Margreatt, daughter of Christ. and Edeth
- 11th November 1674: Thomas, son of Christopher and Edeth

I also found these burials at Sherborne Abbey:

- 29th February 1687/8: Christopher Oliver, uxoratus (married)
- 16th October 1710: Edith Oliver, widow

Christopher Oliver Sr left a will dated the 26th October 1687 (Fig. 30), stating his occupation as a 'victualler' (I subsequently discovered the name of the inn in question was the White Horse). Here is a section of his will in which bequests were made to some members of Christopher's family:

...*"Item I give to my daughter Elizabeth Leach one shilling Item I give to my son William Oliver one shilling Item I give unto my daughter Anne Walter one shilling Item I give unto my daughter Edith Oliver five pounds to be payd her by my son Christopher Oliver within the space of one Year after my decease Item I give to my daughter Joane Oliver five pounds to be payd her at her attaining to the full age of one and twenty yeares by my son Christopher Item I give to my daughter Katherine Oliver Tenn pounds to be paid her at her*

Figure 30: Christopher Oliver's will, 1687

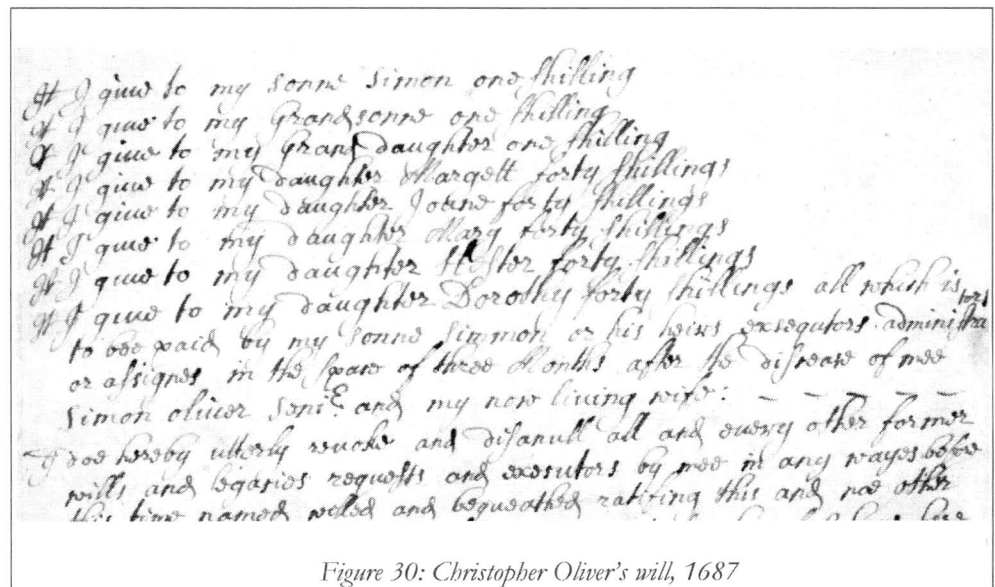

attaining to the age of one and twenty years Item I give to my daughter Margarett Oliver Tenn pounds to be paid her at her attaining to the age of one and twenty years to be likewise payd by my said son Christopher Item I give to my son Thomas Oliver Tenn pounds to be paid him at his attaining to the age of one and twenty years by my said son Christopher Oliver Item I give to my son John Oliver Tenn pounds to be paid him at his attaining to the age of one and twenty years by my said son Christopher Oliver In consideracon whereof and of the sd legacies so to be pd by my sd son Christopher as aforesayd I do hereby give devise and bequeath to my sd son Christopher Oliver All that my now dwelling house and Apptnances with the Garden and backside thereto belonging situate in Sherborne aforesd in a place there called the Green To have and to hold to the sd Christopher Oliver my son his Heires and Assigns from and Immediately after the decease of Edith my wife forever with all deeds evidences and writings whatsoever touching the same…".

This will confirms that Christopher Oliver's wife Edith was alive in 1688. Christopher named his children, probably in order of their age: Elizabeth (married to Mr Leach), William, Anne (married to Mr Walter), Edith, Christopher, Joane (under 21), Katherine (under 21), Margarett (under 21), Thomas (under 21) and John. Marie may have died young as she was not mentioned; Elizabeth, William, Anne and Edith were probably born between their parent's marriage in 1654 and Christopher's birth in ~1664 and John was baptised on the 19th August 1677. Like his father, son Thomas may have become a victualler since there is a will of Thomas Oliver, victualler, dated the 14th July 1718.

Christopher Oliver the elder may well have been the son of Christopher and Margaret Oliver; a child of that name was baptised in Sherborne in 1627 and also of the same parents are: Simon (bp. 1636) and William (bp. 1639) Christopher's brothers. I have found out very little about William, other than that he married a Mary Ridout in 1684, when both of them had been widowed. I don't know the identity of this Mary Ridout, but I found more information about Simon.

Simon Oliver (1636-1699)

Simon Oliver married Dorothy UDALL, daughter of Lionel (an innkeeper in Sherborne) possibly at some point before 1660, and they had several children (baptisms & burials in Sherborne are shown below). Simon was buried in Sherborne on the 2nd August 1699 'uxoratus'; Dorothy Oliver was buried on the 13th August 1713.

- Dorothy (21st August 1660 – 5th February 1674)
- Joane (25th February 1663 – 19th September 1667)
- Margreat (19th March 1666 – alive in 1699)
- Marie (31st October 1671 – alive in 1699)
- Lynell (15th August 1677 – ?)
- Dorothy (2nd June 1678 alive in 1699)
- Elizabeth (27th December 1680 – 29th Sep 1685)

Simon wrote his will on 29th July 1699, just five days before his burial. He left money to his wife Dorothy, to his son Simon, a grandson and granddaughter (presumably the younger Simon's children) and his daughters Margaret, Joane, Mary, Hester and Dorothy. The will was witnessed by Joseph Ridoutt (the only such named individual I have found in the Sherborne parish records was the son of a Thomas and Dorothy Ridout, baptised in 1666). I have not found baptisms in Sherborne for Hester or Simon (but the 1677 Sherborne Manor Survey suggests that he was born in 1663); Lionel wasn't mentioned by his father and so may have died before 1699.

Simon Oliver (1663-1738)

The younger Simon Oliver married Margaret Ridout on the 26th May 1691 in Sherborne. One online transcription of this marriage gives Margaret the middle name of Driscoll but this is not shown in the parish register of Sherborne and hence this information is unsourced and may be inaccurate. [Intriguingly, one candidate for Margaret may have been the daughter of John Ridout and Elizabeth Oliver, baptised in Sherborne on the 26th December 1664.]

Simon and Margaret Oliver had the following children baptised:

- 5th May 1692: Elizabeth, daughter of Simon and Margrett
- 26th December 1694: Simon, son of Simon and Margaret
- 17th February 1694/95: Elizabeth, daughter of Simon and Margrett
- 29th August 1698: Betty, daughter of Symon and Margaret
- 13th January 1700/01: Dorothy, daughter of Simon and Margaret
- 19th July 1703: Ann, daughter of Simon and Margaret
- 15th September 1708: Lionel, son of Simon and Margaret

Simon was buried on the 1st September 1738; I couldn't find a burial for his wife Margaret.

Simon Oliver (1694-1741)

There are two burials in Sherborne Abbey…

- 6th Apr 1739: Ann, wife of Simon was buried
- 29th Sep 1741: Simon Oliver was buried

…and mentions of the following children:

- 30th Dec 1736: Ann daughter of Simon & Ann was baptised
- 28th Feb 1736/37: Ann, daughter of Simon & Ann was buried
- 13th Jul 1738: Lionel, son of Simon & Anne was baptised
- 1st Sep 1738: a male child of Simon Oliver was buried
- 31st Jul 1738: Elizabeth daughter of Simon & Anne was buried

This sad list suggests that Simon Oliver the younger's son Simon (bp. 1694) married a lady called Ann and, within three years, had lost her and three children. His will, dated 25th September 1741, witnessed by Dorothy and Ann Oliver (more than likely his sisters) showed that Simon was a mercer (merchant) by trade and perhaps had just one surviving child, a son Simon:

"I Simon Oliver of Sherborne…. give and devise to my Brother Lionel Oliver and to my Brother in law Charles Vie to their heirs and assigns all my lands tenements and hereditaments whatsoever and wheresoever whereof I have any power to dispose and I do give and bequeath unto the said Lionel Oliver and Charles Vie their executors and administrators all my goods and chattels whatsoever and wheresoever and I make and ordain them executors of this my last will and testament….. I give to my said Brother Lionel Oliver ffive Guineas I give to my said Brother in Law Charles Vie ffive Guineas. I give to my Servant Mary Stacy Two Guineas to buy her Mourning…. and the Residue of my personal estate to my Son Simon Oliver his Heirs Executors and Administrators and my will is that if my said son Simon when he shall attain the age of twenty-one years he shall pay or secure to the satisfaction of my said Trustees and Executors and the survivor of them such of my Debts and Legacies as shall then remain unpaid…" (probate: 14th November 1741).

Simon's sister Betty (bp. 1698) married Charles VIE on the 4th May 1726 at Thornford, four miles SW of Sherborne. Their daughter, Jane (aka Jenny) was baptised on the 11th April 1727 in Sherborne after which the family may have moved. Simon mentioned Jane in his will *("I give to my niece Jenny, daughter of the said Charles Vie, five guineas")*. Jane married James Ridout, probably before 1750. James was a draper by trade and I write more of him in a later chapter. Overleaf (Fig. 31) is a summary of the descendants of Christopher Oliver and Margaret BALLE or BAILIE, who marrried in 1625.

In conclusions, regardless of whether John Ridout married an Oliver lady or not, it is clear that the two families are closely linked over a few generations. James Ridout is of particular interest to me and was included in a family tree by Arthur Ridout (Ridout book page 40). James was a draper by trade and his shop was in Cheap Street, the main commercial thoroughfare in Sherborne. In the next chapter James' history is elaborated, the Olivers make another appearance and North Wootton Ridouts are explored, starting with James' grandfather Thomas (b. 1682).

```
(i) Christopher OLIVER (1627-1688) = Edith RIDOUT (m. 1654)
    (ii) Elizabeth
    (ii) William
    (ii) Anne
    (ii) Edith
    (ii) Christopher (bp. 1664)
    (ii) Marie (bp. 1666)
    (ii) Joan (bp. 1667)
    (ii) Katherine (bp. 1670)
    (ii) Margaret (bp. 1672)
    (ii) Thomas (bp. 1674)
    (ii) John (bp. 1677)
(i) Simon OLIVER (bp. 1636-1699) = Dorothy UDALL (m. ~1660)
    (ii) Simon (bn ~1663-1738) = Margaret RIDOUT (m. 1691)
        (iii) Betty (bp. 1698) = Charles VIE
            (iv) Jane VIE = James RIDOUT
        (iii) Dorothy (bp. 1701)
        (iii) Ann (bp. 1703)
        (iii) Lionel (bp. 1708)
        (iii) Simon (1694-1741) = Ann(e)
            (iv) Simon
    (ii) Joan (bp. 1663)
    (ii) Dorothy (bp. 1666)
    (ii) Margaret (bp. 1666)
    (ii) Marie (bp. 1671)
    (ii) Lionel (bp. 1677)
    (ii) Dorothy (bp. 1678)
    (ii) Elizabeth (bp. 1680)
    (ii) Joane
    (ii) Hester
```

Figure 31: Descendants of Christopher and Margaret OLIVER

17. The Ridouts of North Wootton

Thomas Ridout was baptised in North Wootton on the 13th February 1682, son of Thomas and Margrett. On the 29th March 1718, in Sherborne Abbey, Thomas married Susannah daughter of 'John Porter of Compton' (she was bp. 18th March 1693 in Nether Compton, a village three miles west of Sherborne). I did wonder whether John Porter could possibly be the brother of Elizabeth Porter who married John Ridout of Nethercombe, but I have no evidence one way or the other.

One useful way to discover something of an individual is by looking at his or her will. Both Thomas and Susannah wrote quite detailed wills – first an abridged version of Thomas's will, dated the 14th April 1758:

"In the Name of God Amen I Thomas Ridout of North Wootton in the County of Dorset yeoman being weak but of a sound and disposing mind, memory and understanding do make this my last Will and Testament in manner following. Whereas I have a Mortgage on George Hockey's estate lying in the Parish of Mudford in the County of Somerset for securing the sum of two hundred and thirty Pounds and interest now I do hereby give the said two hundred and thirty Pounds unto my two Sons John Ridout and James Ridout upon Trust that they or the survivor of them shall from the time of my decease pay over unto my daughter Susanna the Wife of Soloman Andrews the Yearly Interest or Produce thereof for the rest of her natural Life for her own private use and separate and apart from her Husband and her Receipt alone shall be a sufficient discharge for the same and from and after her decease I give and bequeath the said Principal sum of two hundred and thirty Pounds unto my Grandchildren Temperance Andrews Thomas Andrews William Andrews Richard Andrews John Andrews Susanah Andrews equally to be divided between them. Also I give unto my said son James Ridout All my freehold Lands and Tenements lying in the parish of Yetminster in the said County of Dorsett to hold to him his executors administrators and assigns for and during all my Estate Term and Interest therein. Also I nominate and appoint my said son James Ridout to be the Lords next Tenant to all my Customary hold estates lying in the parish of Yetminster aforesaid. ... Also I give unto my said wife my Bed Bedstead and ffurniture thereto belonging in the Middle Chamber of the House where I now live. Also I give unto my daughter Elizabeth Ridout one Guinea. Also I give and bequeath unto my Grandson Thomas Ridout son of the said James Ridout my leasehold tenement in North Wootton aforesaid where I now live to hold to him from and immediately after the several deaths of my said Wife Susanah Ridout and of my son John Ridout for and during

all my then remainder of the Term therein. Also I give unto my said Grandson Thomas Ridout one half part of all my household Goods immediately after the death of my said son John Ridout. Lastly all the Rest of my Goods Chattels mortgages stock of cattle debts bonds sum and sums of money and not hereinbefore bequeathed I give unto my said son John Ridout whom I make and constitute sole Executor of this my last Will and Testament ... Witnesses thereto on the presence of the said Testator. John Bulster, Ann Bell, John Fooks."

Thomas was buried at North Wootton (Fig. 32) on the 27th March 1760. His will was proved at London the 20th October of that year. This is an abridged version of Thomas's wife Susannah's will dated the 26th May 1764:

Figure 32: St Peter's church, North Wootton © Aidan Simons

"By this my last Will and Testament made the twenty sixth day of May in the Year of our Lord One thousand and seven hundred and sixty four, I Susannah Ridout of North Wootton in the County of Dorset Widow Do Give and Dispose of my Goods and Effects in Manner following (that is to say) I Give and Bequeath unto my two Sons John Ridout and James Ridout And to the Survivor of them his Executor and Administrators the sum of One Hundred pounds Upon Trust that they the said John Ridout and James Ridout Do as soon as conveniently may be after my Decease place one the Same at Interest on such Security or Securitys as they shall think fitt And pay over such Interest as they shall make thereof unto my Daughter Susannah the wife of Soloman Andrews for the sole and seperate Use During the terme of her natural Life whose receipt alone shall be a sufficient Discharge for the same

And from and after the Decease of the said Susannah Andrews I Give and Bequeath the said sum of One Hundred Pounds in manner following (that is to say) To my Grandaughter Temperance Andrews the Sum of Forty Pounds part thereof And To my Grandaughters Susannah Andrews Elizabeth Andrews and Sarah Andrews the Sum of Twenty Pounds apiece being the residue thereof to be paid them by my said Sons when they shall think proper for the better preferment in Life after they shall Attain their respective Ages of Twenty one ... To my Grandaughter Susannah Ridout the Sum of Forty Pounds part thereof And to my Grandaughters Elizabeth Ridout Jane Ridout and Mary Ridout the Sum of Twenty Pounds a piece being the residue thereof to be paid them by the said Son James Ridout when he shall think proper for the better preferment in Life after they shall attain their respective Ages of Twenty one Years... Also I Give unto my Grandaughter Susannah Noake the Sum of Twenty pounds which I direct to be paid to my Son-in-Law John Noake immediately after my Decease to be by him Applied and Improved for the Benefit of the said Susannah Noake during her Minority And when she shall Arrive to the Age of Twenty one Years I do hereby order and direct that the said John Noake shall pay the said Twenty Pounds with such Interest as he shall make thereof in case he shall then think her deserving of the same And also I Give unto my Daughter Elizabeth the wife of the said John Noake the Sum of Five Pounds. Lastly all the Rest & Residue of my Goods Chattles and Effects I Give and Bequeath unto my said Sons John Ridout and James Ridout whom I make and appoint joint Executors of this my Will In Witness whereof I Susannah Ridout the Testatrix have hereunto Set my Hand & Seal the day & Year above written. Signed Sealed published & Declared by me Susannah Ridout as for her last Will & Testament in the presence of John Glover, John Fooks."

Susannah was buried at North Wootton on the 3rd November 1766; her will was proved in 1767. From these wills, and from parish records, it was possible to identify the following children of Thomas and Susannah:

- John bp. 2nd May 1719 at North Wootton; buried there on the 4th June 1787
- Susannah bp. 6th February 1720 at N. Wootton; married Solomon ANDREWS of Preston on the 25th January 1742 at N. Wootton.
- Thomas bp. 15th October 1725 at N. Wootton; buried on the 4th January 1743.
- James bp. 30th April 1730 at N. Wootton; married Jane daughter of Charles Vie at some point before about 1750; died on the 6th October 1766 and was buried at Folke four days later, on the 10th.
- Elizabeth bp. 27th December 1734 at N. Wootton; married John NOAKE of Wraxall at North Wootton on the 30th Oct 1758.

The oldest son John outlived his brother James and left a will, written on the 24th January 1780:

"I John Ridout of Northwootton in the County of Dorset yeoman do make this my last will and testament in manner and form following that is to say ffirst I do hereby nominate my nephew Charles Ridout of the City of Bristol to be the Lord's next tenant to all that my customary held tenement and estate situate lying and being in the manor of Yetminster in the County of Dorset also I give and bequeath unto my two nephews James Ridout and John Ridout the sum of two hundred pounds apiece to be paid them at their respective ages of twenty one years... Also I give and bequeath unto my said three nieces Betty Ridout Susannah Ridout and Mary Ridout the sum of one hundred pounds apiece to be paid them when they shall attain their respective ages of twenty one years... Also I give to my nephew John Andrews the sum of twenty pounds. Also I give to his Brothers and Sisters the sum of one Guinea each. Also I give to each of the children of my sister Elizabeth Noake one Guinea. Also I give and bequeath unto my nephew Thomas Ridout all my Messuages Lands Tenements and Hereditaments situate lying and being at Holwell or elsewhere in the County of Somerset to hold to him his heirs and assigns forever but charged with the payment of all my Debts and Legacies herein before given. Lastly all my Leasehold Estates and also all the rest and residue of my Personal Estates and Effects of what nature or kind soever I give and bequeath unto my said Nephew Thomas Ridout whom I appoint and make sole executor of this my will... witnesses hereto John Fooks, Charles B Hart, Thomas Trevellon."

This will was proved at London on the 27th October 1787 and shows that John was probably not married or, had he been so, then was widowed and without surviving children at the time of his decease. From these wills it can be seen that the majority of property of the three adults was ultimately left to Thomas and Susannah's grandson Thomas, oldest son of James Ridout, who received a tenement in North Wootton from his grandfather (after the death of his grandmother and uncle John) and all the tenements in Holwell 'and elsewhere in Somerset' from his uncle.

James Ridout 'the yeoman' (1730-1766)

John's younger brother James appeared in various Sherborne records and hence I know a little about him. James's wife Jane was, as stated beforehand, the daughter of Charles Vie and Betty Oliver. Betty wrote a will on the 14th December 1773 (probate August 1777) leaving her dwelling house in Sherborne, which she had purchased from her nephew, Simon Oliver, first to her unmarried daughter Elizabeth Vie then, after her decease, to her grandson Charles (Vie) Ridout, son of James (by then deceased). Betty also bequeathed her interest in another property in Cold Harbour, Sherborne to James's son Thomas and a third to James's daughter Elizabeth. Monetary bequests were made to all of James's children and gifts of plate and clothes went to Charles Vie and Elizabeth, probably the two oldest grandchildren. Betty named her 'shopman' as James Andrews (perhaps a relative of Solomon Andrews?) meaning that Betty had probably kept a shop in the town; her husband was a yeoman farmer. This will, and various parish records, show that James and Jane Ridout had ten children including sons Charles Vie (bp. 15th May 1764 at Folke) and James (bp. 18th January 1765 at Folke), both of whom became involved in the linen and drapery business:

James Ridout wrote a will dated 3rd October 1760, which I obtained from Dorset Record Office:

"In the Name of God Amen I James Ridout of Folke in the County of Dorset Yeoman being sick and weak but of sound and disposing mind memory and understanding do make this my last Will and testament in manner following First I nominate and Appoint my Brother John Ridout of North Wootton in the County of Dorset Yeoman and William Horsey of Folke aforesaid Clerk to be the Lord's next Tenants to all my Customary held Tenements and Lands lying and being in the Manor of Yetminster in the said County of Dorset In Trust that they shall sell and Dispose thereof And the Moneys arising therefrom to place out at Interest in their Names And in the Names of my other Trustee hereinafter named upon such Security or Securities as they shall think fitt and Apply the Interest and produce thereof to and for the Maintenance and Education of all my Children in Equal Shares and Proportions during their respective Minorities And from and after my said Children shall attain their respective Ages of Twenty two years My Wish is That the Principal Sum shall go and be divided amongst my said Children in Manner following that is to say Three parts thereof to my sons and Two parts to my Daughters. Also I give unto my Wife Jane Ridout the Sum of Two Hundred pounds of lawfull money of Great Britain to be paid her by my Executors hereinafter named within Six Months next after my Decease Also all my Stock, Moneys, Goods, Chattles and other my Personal Estate of what nature or kind soever I Give and Bequeath unto my said Brother John Ridout, William Horsey and also Jonathan Cadie the Younger of Holwell in the County of Somerset Yeoman and James Beeke of Oborne in the County of Dorset yeoman In Trust that they or the Survivors or Survivor of them do and shall with all Convenient speed after my decease Sell and Dispose of all my Stock, Cattle, Implements of Husbandry and out of the moneys arising therefrom after payment of the Said Two Hundred pounds to my said Wife… Also I do hereby appoint the said John Ridout William Horsey Jonathan Cadie and James Noake Executors of this my Will in Trust for the purposes before mentioned. In Witness whereof I have hereunto sett my

hand and seal the third day of October in the year of our Lord One Thousand Seven Hundred & Sixty."

[Signed by James Ridout, Elizabeth Vie and John Fookes; mark of Martha Perrott. Probate at Sherborne on the 9th September 1767.]

Charles Vie Ridout, son of James and Jane (1753-1815)

Baptised on the 15th May 1753 at Folke, nearly four miles SE of Sherborne, James's son Charles Vie went to Bristol as a young man, perhaps because it was such a bustling port and he was in the Irish linen trade. His name appeared in the Bristol Burgess Books of 1781 and, much later, in the voter's list for the General Election of 1812. On the 18th October 1784 at St Lawrence Jewry and St Mary Magdalene in London, Charles married sixteen-year old Jane SMITH with the permission of her guardian. Interestingly, in a marriage settlement between the couple, the trustees were named as Jane's mother-in-law Clare Blyth, a clothier, and Thomas Ridout of North Wootton, Charles's grandfather but, after Thomas and Charles had died, the role was taken on by 'John Ridout of New Bridge Street, Blackfriars in London' (John Gibbs Ridout, uncle of Thomas Gibbs Ridout). In a twenty year period, between 1786 and 1806, the couple had twelve children.

Street directories of 1793-94 show that Charles was a partner in a family drapery business 'Oliver, Ridout & Oliver', which was located at 1 High Street and also as 'linen merchants' in Maryport Street, Bristol. An entry dated the 23rd February 1795 in the London Gazette (p.1456) records the theft of silk and cotton handkerchiefs from the shop by a young female. The goods, worth 10s, were 'the property of Simon Oliver, Charles Ridout and Lionel Oliver, partners in the said shop of Simon Oliver at the parish of All Saints' (Bristol). In the last chapter I wrote about various Simon Olivers – the one mentioned here was probably the only surviving child of the youngest Simon (1694-1741) and his wife Ann(e).

On the 21st December 1805, a notice was posted in the Staffordshire Advertiser and published in the London Gazette (Fig. 33) that a company partnership in Wales had been dissolved, three members having left. I was intrigued to see that Charles Ridout and Simon Oliver, with others, had been involved with a grocery business at Hirwaun in South Wales. The Rhondda Cynon Taff Society records: "In 1803 the (Hirwaun iron-) works passed (from Thomas Bacon) to a new partnership of Francis William Bouzer, Simon Oliver,

Lionel Oliver and Jeremiah Homfray. Homfray later retired and was replaced by George Overton. After 1805 this partnership began a program of work at the site which included the construction of a second blast furnace. Unfortunately, the construction of a second furnace was not enough to save the works from a trade depression and the works were put up for sale again in 1813." The London Gazette, a few years later (January 1813), printed bankruptcy notices naming, amongst others, Lionel Oliver (http://www.london-gazette.co.uk/issues/15864/pages/1456/page.pdf)

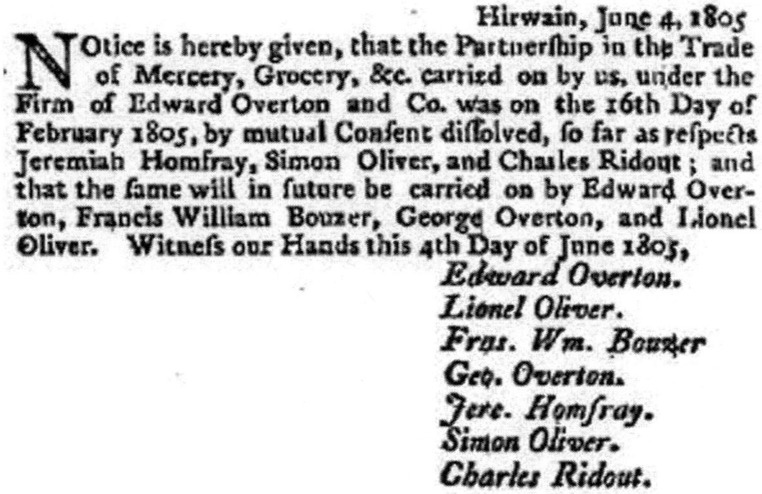

> Hirwain, June 4, 1805
>
> Notice is hereby given, that the Partnership in the Trade of Mercery, Grocery, &c. carried on by us, under the Firm of Edward Overton and Co. was on the 16th Day of February 1805, by mutual Consent diffolved, fo far as refpects Jeremiah Homfray, Simon Oliver, and Charles Ridout; and that the fame will in future be carried on by Edward Overton, Francis William Bouzer, George Overton, and Lionel Oliver. Witnefs our Hands this 4th Day of June 1805,
>
> *Edward Overton.*
> *Lionel Oliver.*
> *Fras. Wm. Bouzer*
> *Geo. Overton.*
> *Jere. Homfray.*
> *Simon Oliver.*
> *Charles Ridout.*

Figure 33: Public notice, London Gazette 1805

I subsequently found a will for Simon Oliver, dated 20th May 1814 which was proved two months later; he wrote that Lionel, his son had been declared bankrupt (with respect to Hirwaun) and still owed him many thousands of pounds; for this reason he excluded him from his bequests. Simon left a small sum of money to his partner, Charles Ridout.

Charles Vie Ridout died from apoplexy and was buried, aged 63, on the 1st March 1815 at St. Michael's Church in Bristol. It is probable that Simon and Charles continued their Bristol shop until their respective deaths and may have been only sleeping partners at Hirwaun.

Charles lived at the Royal Fort, a rather imposing building which now houses Bristol University's Centre for Advanced Studies (Fig. 34). On Sunday 2nd February 1812, he was visited at the Fort by a young Canadian, Thomas Gibbs Ridout (grandson of George Ridout, baker of Sherborne), who was staying in Bristol for a few days as part of a tour of England. It seems probable that Thomas Gibbs, who had never been to Britain before, was given instructions by his father Thomas on which family members he should visit in England (see Chapter 10) since he almost certainly didn't run into Charles or James by accident!

Figure 34: The Royal Fort, Bristol

James Ridout, younger brother of Charles Vie (1765-1836)

Charles Vie Ridout's younger brother James, baptised on the 18th January 1765 at Folke, also became a draper; perhaps the business came down through Betty Vie. James's shop was at The Parade in Cheap Street, Sherborne – today the busy main thoroughfare of the town. Below is the wording of an advertisement published by the Sherborne Mercury on Monday the 28th May 1792:

"James Ridout, Cheap-street, Sherborne, grateful to his friends for past favours, solicits their inspection of his new purchases, lately made in London, and which will be sold on the lowest terms, particularly Dimittys, Muslinettes, and White Calicoes, at very reduced prices; a great variety of Genteel Prints; Muslins of every description; an assortment of Fancy Waistcoatings, and other Articles of Dress for Gentleman's Wear; also a good assortment of Men's and Boy's Hats. Light gold taken in exchange for goods, without any deductions. N.B. Funerals completely furnished."

It is not clear at what point James started the business in Cheap St but the advertisement implies that he was not new (reference to 'past favours') and yet he was just twenty-seven in 1792.

On the 9th June 1796, James married Susanna PARSONS, daughter of the Rev. Francis Parsons of Yeovil and the sister of the Rev. John Parsons, Vicar of Sherborne. By the time Susanna reached the age of thirty-nine, she had borne James nine children.

Evidently James was an upright citizen of Sherborne since, as well as being a Burgess, in 1799 he became first a Governor then the Warden of Sherborne School; he was also Warden in 1815, 1821 and 1833. According to the school's own website, in 1823 the number of pupils, in what was then King Edward (VI)'s free grammar school, was as low as eighteen (two less than the number reported by Thomas Ridout eleven years earlier!) but, by 1845 under the headship of the Rev. Ralph LYON, numbers had steadily increased to reach 150 before declining again. Sherborne achieved independent public school status in 1871 and today is a very prestigious institution.

In Piggott's directories of 1823 and 1830, at Sherborne, James's shop is entered as 'James Ridout & Son, Cheap St' and (only in 1830) also 'Sams & Ridout, Long St.' Interestingly, under Wines & Spirits Merchants, James is again listed as Ridout, James & Son (British only) Cheap St.'

Whether as a result of his business acumen or because of bequests from family members over the years, James acquired a lovely home called Abbey Grange (Fig. 35) then referred to as the Abbey Barn, it having been converted from the central part of the old monastery barn in 1828. On a visit to Sherborne a few years ago, I found the house and was delighted when the owners allowed me into the grounds to photograph the exterior. The back garden reached the rear of the shops in Cheap Street and I was pretty sure that this had afforded a very pleasant shortcut to work for James!

Figure 35: Abbey Grange, Sherborne

James died in Folke and was buried on the 9th September 1836, Susannah died 20th February 1846. James left a lengthy will, dated 25th April 1836, which is much condensed here:

"This is the last will and testament of me James Ridout of Sherborne in the county of Dorset, mercer and draper, whereby I dispose of the worldly estate wherewith it hath pleased God to bestow me in manner and form following, that is to say that first I give Susannah my dear wife all the household goods and furniture, plate, linen, china, books, pictures and liquors of all kinds that may be found in or about the dwelling house and premises where I am now or may be dwelling at the time of my decease… also I give and devise the messuage or dwelling house … situate on the Parade in Cheap Street Sherborne and with all the fixtures of the same whether for trade or otherwise to my son James and to his heirs and assignees for ever but chargeable with the payment of an annuity of twenty pounds… to my brother John during the term of his natural life… and I likewise bequeath to my son James all the household goods and furniture plate, linen and china and all the liquors which shall be found at the time of my decease but no part of my stock in trade as that I intend he shall take by purchase at a valuation as hereinafter… to my four daughters I give my pew in the Sherborne Church… whereas my life stands insured in the Equitable Office for the sum of one thousand pounds… and the accumulations which have been added I believe amount to nearly the same … now I give and bequeath the aid policy and all additions and accumulations…unto my four daughters in equal shares also I bequeath to my son Charles the sum of five hundred pounds payable at the decease of his Mother… I bequeath a policy which I have with the Royal Exchange … for the sum of three

hundred pounds and all benefit to… unto and equally bequeath my sons James and Charles and my daughter Fanny and as to the messuage or dwelling house and premises wherein I now reside called "Abbey Barns" with the freehold, brasshouse, stable, outhouses and garden thereto adjoining and also the freehold messuage or dwelling house garden and premises next adjoining and now rented of me by Mrs Eastham I give and devise the same unto my esteemed friend the Reverend Ralph Lyon master of the King's School in Sherborne aforesaid and to his heirs executors and administrators… and suffer my dear wife to have hold and enjoy the same and to receive and have the income and profits thereof to her own use and absolutely during her life she keeping the same in proper repair and from and immediately after her death then upon trust that the said Ralph Lyon, his heirs, executors or administrators do and shall absolutely sell and dispose of all the said houses and premises by public auction or by private… make payment of a legacy of ten pounds to my shopman Richard Ffoot if living with me at the time of my decease as a mark of my regard for his faithful services… the said Ralph Lyon his executors and administrators shall allow my son James who will succeed me in my business to become the purchaser of the whole or any part of my stock in trade as mercer and draper."

Proved at London 14th December 1836 before the Judge by the oath the Reverend Ralph Lyon, Doctor in Divinity, the sole executor to whom administration was granted having first sworn by commission duly to administer.

Links between North Wootton and Sherborne Ridouts

I have already described that Thomas Gibbs Ridout visited both Charles and James Ridout in their respective home towns of Bristol and Sherborne during the year 1812. His narrative does not inform us of the nature of their relationship but the lack of intimacy in Thomas's description does not infer that he felt in any way close to these older men. As stated earlier, Thomas Gibbs Ridout was the grandson of George Ridout the baker. George died in October 1786 and interestingly, James was involved in the administration of his estate. Below is the signature from that document; James would have been 23:

This is the signature of James Ridout on his marriage to Susannah Parsons on the 9th June 1796...... which appears to me to be similar in some respects to the first signature ten years earlier.

Another co-administrator of George Ridout's estate was Charles Bull HART, who also witnessed the will of James's brother John Ridout of North Wootton in 1787 (see above). Hart married Elizabeth Vie on the 11th October 1776; Elizabeth was sister of Jane Vie and therefore Charles was James Ridout Junior's uncle. Charles died in 1805 and bequeathed a great deal of his estate to his late wife's nephews and nieces, including Sherborne properties and £1,000 to James, £500 each to Charles Vie and John and other bequests to their sisters Susannah and Elizabeth. One of Hart's executors was Thomas Ridout, gentleman of Seaborough, Somerset brother of James and Charles Vie; Hart left money to Thomas's daughter Elizabeth.

I started this chapter by stating that Thomas Ridout (1682-1760) was the son of Thomas and Margrett and was baptised in North Wootton. However, Arthur Ridout recorded Thomas's baptism as the 21st April 1694 in Sherborne and that the father, also Thomas (1668-1694), was the son of John Ridout and his wife Alice (née Toogood) [Ridout book, page 7]. However, as stated in Chapter 14, I believe that John and Alice's son Thomas was a cordwainer, baptised in 1667, who went to London, married twice, had a family and died in 1734.

```
                    ?
                    |
        Thomas (b. ?) = Margaret
                    |
        Thomas (bp. 1682) = Susanna Porter
                    |
        James (bp. 1730) = Jane Vie
```

18. Richard of Folke & Richard of North Wootton

In the last chapter I wrote about Thomas Ridout (1682-1760) son of Thomas and Margaret of North Wootton. Arthur Ridout thought the couple had come originally from Sherborne, but I think this Ridout family, for reasons given below, lived exclusively in North Wootton and may have done so for a while. My theory is that Thomas Ridout Sr of North Wootton was the son of a Richard and Jane – but Richard's lineage is hard to pin down, not least of all because at one point there were two Richard Ridouts living at the same time who were possibly the same age!

The puzzle of the two Richards

William Ridowte of Hyle (1553-1620)'s son, Thomas Ridout of North Wootton (bp. 1574) and his second wife Edith PALMER baptised one son Richard on the 24th September 1618 and another on the 19th November 1620. Seeing two children of the same name usually, but not always, implies that the first child died before the baptism of the second; I looked for the burial of an infant Richard between 1618 and 1620 in North Wootton or Sherborne (often the villagers were buried in the larger nearby town) but I failed to find one. Nonetheless, the second Richard evidently survived at least thirty-four years as here is a small extract from the 1654 will of Walter Ridout, another of Thomas's sons:

"Item I give unto Edith Ridout the daughter of Richard my brother of Alweston four pounds… Item I give unto Thomas Ridout the son of Richard Ridout of North Wootton that pte of wood which is between my brother and I at Lillington".

Allweston is in the parish of Folke. The wording indicates that 'Richard of Folke' was Walter's brother but the relationship between Walter and Richard of North Wootton, friend or family, was not elaborated. Lillington is a small village about five miles south of Sherborne, but nearer to North Wootton (see Fig. 36).

Figure 36: 1930 map of Dorset, Lillington (arrow)

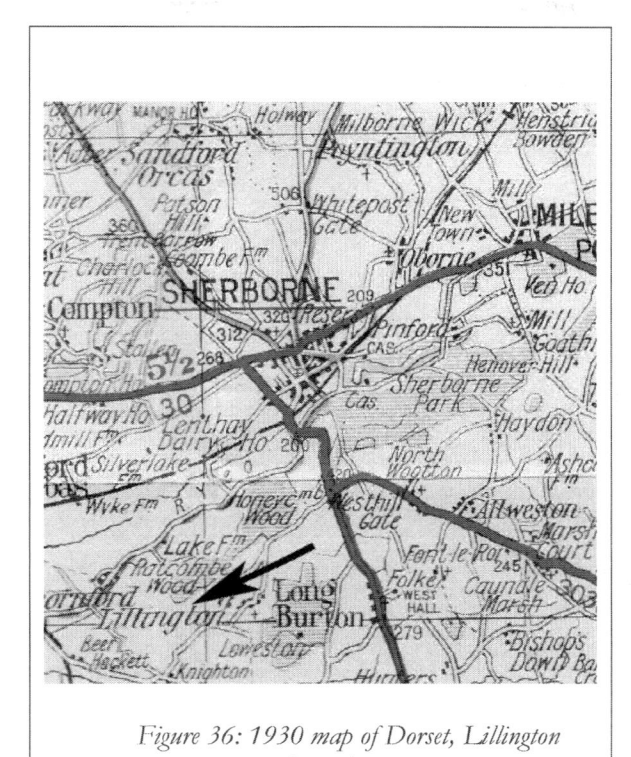

William Ridowte of Hyle also made a bequest to grandson Richard in his will, written on the 9th May 1620. Richard may then either have been an as yet un-baptised newborn or a two year old boy. Whilst unusual, having two children of the same name was not unheard of and was sometimes an insurance against losing property where the named child was one of three 'lives' on a deed. However, Arthur Ridout considered that Richard of Folke and Richard of North Wootton were the same man who simply had property in two villages [Ridout book, page 8] but I am sure that this is not true.….

Richard Ridout of Folke

According to early parish records, Richard Ridout of Folke married Agnes KAINES; their first child, Edith, named by Walter in 1654, was baptised in Folke on the 18th April 1641. The couple had several children over the next few years, the last being Richard (bp. 17th July 1654). Richard Sr was mentioned a few times in manorial records, for example in the Protestation Returns of 1641 (in which a Richard Ridout of North Wootton was also listed), also in Chancery Proceedings, in the case of Bunter vs Downe dated the 11th April 1659, in which Richard was described as a 38 year old yeoman, and in a Court Leet in which Richard was listed as the tythingman (a village spokesperson) for Folke.

Richard died and was buried in Folke churchyard (Fig. 37) on the 6th September 1669. He left a will, the probate of which was granted in 1678 under the authority of the Dean of Sarum (Wilts & Swindon Archive:

P5/1677/41). Richard, a yeoman, appointed his wife Agneta (Agnes) as his sole executrix and bequeathed his daughters Joan, Edith (now Mrs CLARK), Constance, Hannah, Mary, Margaret, Jane, Elner and son Richard 1/- each. The remainder of his estate was left to Agnes; William Fauntleroy was named as overseer and witnessed the will along with Joan Ridout.

Figure 37: St Lawrence's church, Folke (© Chris Downer)

Agnes Ridout died and was buried in Folke on the 13th October 1689. In her will, dated 24th November 1686 and proved in 1690 (Wilts & Swindon: P5/1690/46), she also mentioned her children: Margaret (who received a bed & an old chest), Mary WEST (a hat & 1/-), Edith Clarke, Joan COLLIER, Constance FEANER, Hannah NEWMAN & son Richard, who were given 1/- each. Agnes nominated her daughters Jane & Ellinor to be her executors and her 'loving friends' John Hammond & Richard Bedelcombe to be overseers. The witnesses to the will were John & Mary Hammond. So, as far as can be ascertained, Richard Ridout and Agnes Kaines married, had children, lived, died and were buried – in the village of Folke.

Richard Ridout of North Wootton

Three miles away in the village of North Wootton, another Richard Ridout also appeared in manorial records, for example, in the Chancery Proceedings (Dorset Suits No 138/8, Oke v Oke) dated the 29th December 1657 in which it was said that he was a 36 year old husbandman. This Richard Ridout died on the 13th March 1661 and was buried six days later in Sherborne, but he was recorded as being 'of North Wootton'; he died intestate but a document dated the 14th December 1662 shows that the joint administrators of his estate were widow Jeane (a variant of Jean or Jane) Ridout, John Brett and Thomas Ridout.

So, Richard Ridout of North Wootton was married to Jane and was born, according to Chancery records, in ~1621 – roughly the same time as Richard Ridout of Folke, but I'm sure that this is a different man; Richard Ridout of North Wootton died in 1661, not 1669. The document regarding administration of the latter's estate includes an inventory which was compiled by John Brett senior and junior and a Thomas Ridout of North Wootton on the 4th July 1662:

	£	s	d
His wearing apparel	03	00	00
Five oxen	24	00	00
Brown bull and heifers	15	00	00
Five yearlings	05	00	00
Two horses	05	00	00
Five ewes and lambes and four sheepe	03	02	00
One pigge	00	10	00
Eleven hens and one cocke	00	05	00
Twelve bushells of wheate and …	18	00	00
Twenty bushells of dates	02	00	00
Three bushells of pease	00	12	00
Two sides of bacon	01	00	00
For corn that was not threshed	01	13	04
For three brasse potts	00	15	00
Three brass pans, three kittles, two skillets	02	00	00
14 pewter dishes, one candlestick, one salte	01	00	00
Two featherbeds and two down beds	01	15	00
4 bedsteads and the cloathes for fower beds	02	04	00
Two table boards and 6 joynt stooles	01	00	00
Four barrels	00	08	00
Fower trendles, other timber vessels	00	13	04
Two cubardes and two iron …	00	06	00
Two table clothes and six napkins	00	06	00
Two yoakes and one chain … (illegible)	05	00	00
(illegible)	00	13	00

| For lumber | 00 | 05 | 00 |

Signed by John Brett, John Brett and Thomas Ridout (who made his mark 'R').

The 1677 Sherborne Manor Survey shows in the homage of North Wootton a copyholder Jane Ridout, a widow aged 63 years (b. ~1614) and her sons Thomas (aged 23, b. ~1654) and John (aged 21 years, b. ~1656). The property in question was a 'tenement with the appurtenances'; the acreage comprised 24 acres of pasture land, 13 of arable and 6 of meadow (total 43 acres) plus a yard. The annual rent was 10s 9d, with a yearly value of £15 and two capons at Easter. I searched for the baptisms of the two men mentioned in the 1677 survey, Jane's sons Thomas and John. One possible baptism was that of John, on the 8th April 1655 in Sherborne to Richard Ridout.

In the 1709 Manor Survey of Sherborne, in the homage of North Wootton, is shown a copyhold tenement with appurtenances and a yard plus 24 acres of pasture, 6¼ of meadow and 13 of arable land (43¼ acres) with an annual rent of 10s 9d and two capons at Easter. Clearly, this is identical to the tenement described in 1677. The 'lives' are Thomas Ridout (55, b. ~1654), John Ridout his brother (53, b. ~1656) and 'John Ridout his grandson'. The years of birth for the two men are identical to those in 1677 and hence these two 'lives' remained unchanged for over thirty years but, in the interim, Thomas had become not just a father but a grandfather, indicating that one of his children had a son John – the wording does not make it clear who was the boy's father.

In 1717, according to the Sherborne Rentals, Thomas Ridout agreed to 'add one life in reversion of two other lives' for a leasehold tenement in North Wootton and in 1725, 'Thomas Ridout Senior agreed to add the life of John Ridout, nephew of the said Thomas in reversion of him, the said Thomas and John his brother' for a fine (fee) of £30 on his copyhold tenement'. At this point, Thomas would have been seventy-one and his brother John two years younger. The 'nephew John' implies that Thomas's brother, John (or indeed another brother if there was one), had married and had a son John before 1725.

I found burials in the Sherborne registers for both Thomas and his wife Margaret, but not John. Thomas was buried on the 28th June 1727 'of North Wootton' and Margaret two years later on the 22nd May 1729, also in Sherborne 'widow of North Wootton'. Interestingly, there is an entry in the

North Wootton registers showing that a (?this) Thomas Ridout was the churchwarden in 1682 and maybe it was he that corrected the earlier parish register entries relating to Thomas Ridout (b. 1574) by adding Thomas's wife's name 'Edith' retrospectively (Fig. 38):

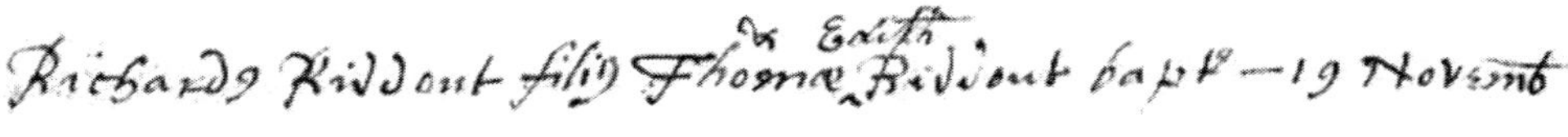

Figure 38: Richard Ridout's baptism in North Wootton, 1620

In 1735, Thomas Ridout 'agreed to purchase by Copy of Court Roll, the Life of James Ridout his son in reversion of John Ridout his Uncle (now aged seventy-nine or possibly recently deceased) and John Ridout another son of the said Thomas Ridout' for £35. Finally, in 1756 Thomas 'added a life and exchanged one' but with no details of individuals. Further alterations to the same copyhold lease of North Wootton were made through the years by 'Mr John Ridout' and, in 1735, it was held by 'He, Jno Ridout son of Thos and Saml Ridout, two sons of Thos Ridout.' Once more the land comprised 43¼ acres with annual value of £15 and rent of 10s 9d and two capons at Easter. Thomas Ridout held two leasehold tenancies in North Wootton and one of the lives was 'Susannah, his wife'.

It can be seen, from the tree at the end of this text that this is the family to which I referred in the last chapter, 'The Ridouts of North Wootton' but that these manor records reveal three new individuals: John (b.~1656) Thomas's brother, Thomas and Margaret's unnamed son and Samuel, son of Thomas Ridout and Susannah.

Tracing the North Wootton copyhold forward in time was intriguing but I also wondered how far back this property had been occupied by Ridouts. In the 1614 Manor Survey, in North Wootton, a copyhold tenancy is described:

"Thomas Ridowte holdeth bt Copie bearinge date the xj th daye of Aprill in the xxxix yeare of [our] late Quene Elizabeth by the grante of Sir Walter Ralegh, one tenemente & a yardelande conteininge a dwelling a barne orcharde garden & backside & a Close of pasture adjoininge conteininge iij acres, ij acres of meadow being in the moore, Close of pasture called Brailande conteining xij acres, j close of pasture called Quyntine conteining j acre & half, one close of pasture lande called Strowde conteining vij acres And in the common field in Parkfield iij acres In the Eastfield iij acres & half And in the southfield vj acres all arable lande, w[i]th comon for xvj beaste && xl sheepe in the comon field Rente"

Translated, Thomas Ridout held a copyright tenancy, dated 15th April 1596 by a grant of Sir Walter Raleigh. The tenement comprised a dwelling house, a yard and land (5 acres meadow, 27 acres of pasture and 6 acres of arable land, total 38 acres). Amazingly, although more than sixty years earlier than the 1677 survey, the rent and annual value were identical and would remain so as late as 1748, when John Ridout 'son of Thomas' was still the copyholder. In 1748, the tenement was again described in detail : 3 Closes called 'Bralaindes' (16 acres), 1 Close called 'Holk Stile' (1 acre), 1 Close called 'Quintons Mead' (¾ acre), 'Cross Field' (3 acres), Orchard (1½ acres), Moor Meadow (3 acres), three pastures 'Strouds' (12 acres) and 'Taylors Close' (¾ acre), totalling 38 acres with the same rent of 10s 9d, largely unchanged from 134 years earlier!

So, a man called Thomas Ridout who was presumably an adult in 1614, if not 1596, held the copyhold tenancy of a farm or smallholding in North Wootton which, at some point in the intervening sixty-three years, passed to Jane Ridout, Richard's widow and her two sons and then to the various descendants of Thomas and Margaret. Perhaps the original tenant was William Ridowte and Agnetha Barnard's son Thomas (b. 1574) and maybe he passed the tenancy to Richard, and thence to Richard's son Thomas and his descendants. This Thomas had probably moved to North Wootton from Sherborne at some point between the baptism of his first child, Mary (bp. 1598 in Sherborne) and that of his second, William (bp. 1599 in N. Wootton) But, is it really likely that Thomas and Edith Palmer named two sons Richard and that both survived into adulthood? Whilst there are precedents to this practice it bothers me that, in 1654, Walter Ridout didn't identify Thomas, son of Richard Ridout of North Wootton as one of his nephews, albeit he left the boy some land, indicating a probable relationship. William Ridowte didn't name two Richards in his 1620 will either, only one being the 'son of my son Thomas', although maybe the second son was as yet unborn. I do wonder, however, if perhaps like the Richards, there were also two Thomas Ridouts living in North Wootton at one time!

It is unfortunate that the parish records for North Wootton are very sparse; some years have no entries at all and this is true of the period 1650-1659 when Richard and Jane may have married and when both Richard's sons Thomas and John might have been baptised (although perhaps it was the correct John who was baptised in Sherborne in 1655). This mystery may remain unsolved, however unsatisfactory and frustrating. Clearly, at some point in history, there were links between Sherborne and North Wootton Ridouts and later, when John Gibbs Ridout was involved with James Ridout's family, this is obviously true. I have described a scenario in which two men called Richard Ridout co-existed in Dorset and were somehow connected but, although I can offer no more evidence than has been written here, I still don't think that Richard Ridout of Sherborne and Richard Ridout of North Wootton were the same man!

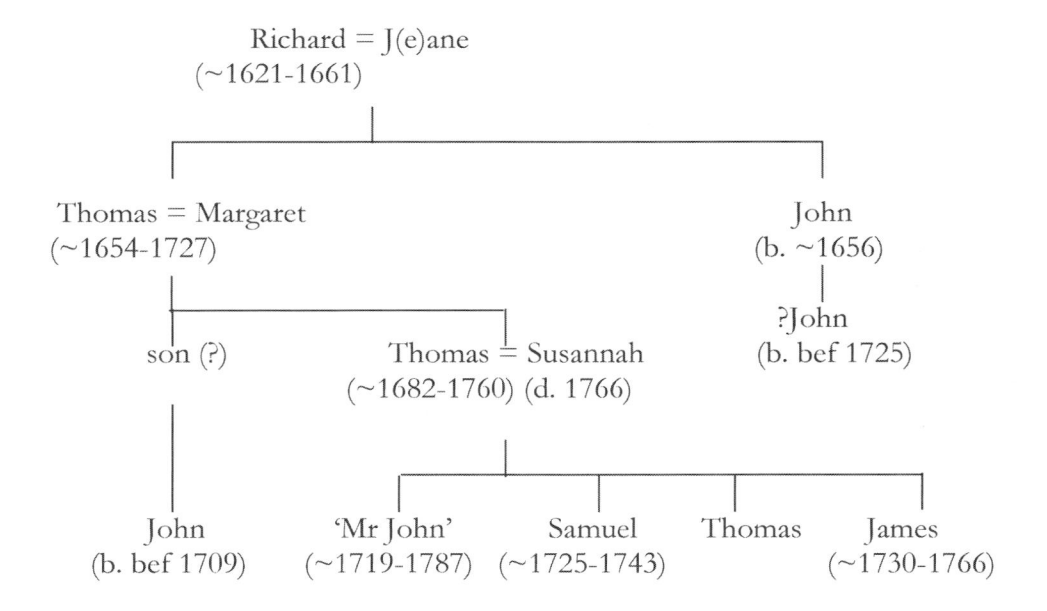

```
                    Richard = J(e)ane
                     (~1621-1661)
                          |
            ┌─────────────┴─────────────┐
    Thomas = Margaret                  John
    (~1654-1727)                    (b. ~1656)
         |                              |
   ┌─────┴─────┐                      ?John
  son (?)   Thomas = Susannah      (b. bef 1725)
          (~1682-1760) (d. 1766)
                |
      ┌─────────┼──────────┬─────────┐
    John    'Mr John'   Samuel   Thomas    James
  (b. bef 1709) (~1719-1787) (~1725-1743)  (~1730-1766)
```

19. William Rydeowte of Chettle: a 16th century gentleman

Family historians consider themselves lucky if they can trace their roots back through a few centuries but many hit a 'brick wall' even within the period of civil registration, so I am very fortunate to have a story to tell as far back as the Tudor times, which is almost certainly when William Rydeowte 'of Chettle' was born. From a document dated 1613, which I will describe later, William's next of kin, brother Thomas, was said to be "fifty years of age or more" when William died (in 1603). If William was a similar age to Thomas, then he was born in ~1553 or before, but then he may have been much older, or indeed younger, than his brother! According to genealogist Arthur Ridout, William's wife was Alice, sister of William Hynton [Ridout book, page 30]; unfortunately, Arthur didn't give a source for this information but I did find a burial at Sherborne on the 30th April 1611: 'Alicia Rideowte widow generosa', meaning that she was the widow of a gentleman. Wikipedia defines a gentleman as 'a man of the lowest rank of the English gentry, standing below an esquire and above a yeoman'. William was likely to have been either the younger son of a younger son of a peer or the younger son of a knight or an esquire.

Of course, I can't be sure that every 16th century record of a man named William Rydeowte in Sherborne alludes to the same individual as the documents bear a wide range of dates. However, during that period, and for a long time thereafter, governance of St John's Almshouse and King Edward VI Free Grammar School in the town generally fell to the same group of gentlemen and hence the mention of William Rydeowte in both contexts probably does refer to one man.

Figure 39: Wax seal of Sherborne School, 16thC

Here follows a short list of documents, most of which I recently examined at Dorset History Centre:

[1] 1555/6: Lease between the warden of Sherborne School (Fig. 39) and William Rydeowte concerning the Great Garden (Litten) on the north side of the schoolhouse and the Plumbhouse, for 13s 4d per annum. [Ref: S235/D1/1/1].

In the fourth year of his short reign, King Edward VI endowed a grammar school in his name at Sherborne to replace the old school which had fallen into disuse at the time of the Dissolution of the Monasteries under Edward's father, Henry VIII. Here is a small part of the Charter, dated 29th March 1550:

"29 die Marcii, Anno Regni Regis Edwardi VI quarto. The kinges maiestie by thadvise of his prevy Counsaill is pleased and contented that a free grammar Scholle shall be erected and established in Shirborne in the Countie of Dorset and Landes to the yerely valueof £20 to be geven and assured by his highness to the mayntenaunce thereof

And that there shall be a Corporacion of 20 of the Inhabytauntes of the Towne and parishe of Shirborne aforesaid to be enabled to have properties [in] succession as governors of the possessions, revenues and goodes of the same Scole, And to have power to Receyve the landes to be appointed for the said Scole, and to have thorder and governance thereof"

A 99-year building lease was granted in 1554-5 for:

"Two houses known as the School House and the Plumbe House with their gardens, a garden called the Abbey Lytten, a garden on the south side of the School House called the School Barton and all the 'voide' land between the east end of the parish church and the School Barton where the chapel of Our Lady the Bowe and the Ankres House were built"

This lease allowed renovation or rebuilding of the Old Schoolhouse (a small building within the grounds of the old monastery), the Plumbhouse (a building where the lead work of the monastery was carried out), Barton (back yard, of a building), Litten (monks' burial ground) and land formerly occupied by two chapels that had been partly demolished. All of these parcels of land, granted to Sir John Horsey by Henry VIII, were leased by him to the school governors on the 25th March 1555 for a fine (fee) of £13 6s 8d and at the annual rent of 13s 4d. Subsequent school accounts show several payments for work involved in re-building and expanding the school. As no tuition fees were charged, renting out lands and buildings in Sherborne and elsewhere provided a much needed income for the new school; as outlined in the charter these properties were gifted to the school by the crown and other benefactors. This document shows that in 1555/6 the governors leased the Great Garden (the Litten) and Plumbhouse to William Rydeowte; I suspect he was named merely as a representative of the Governors of Sherborne School (Fig. 40).

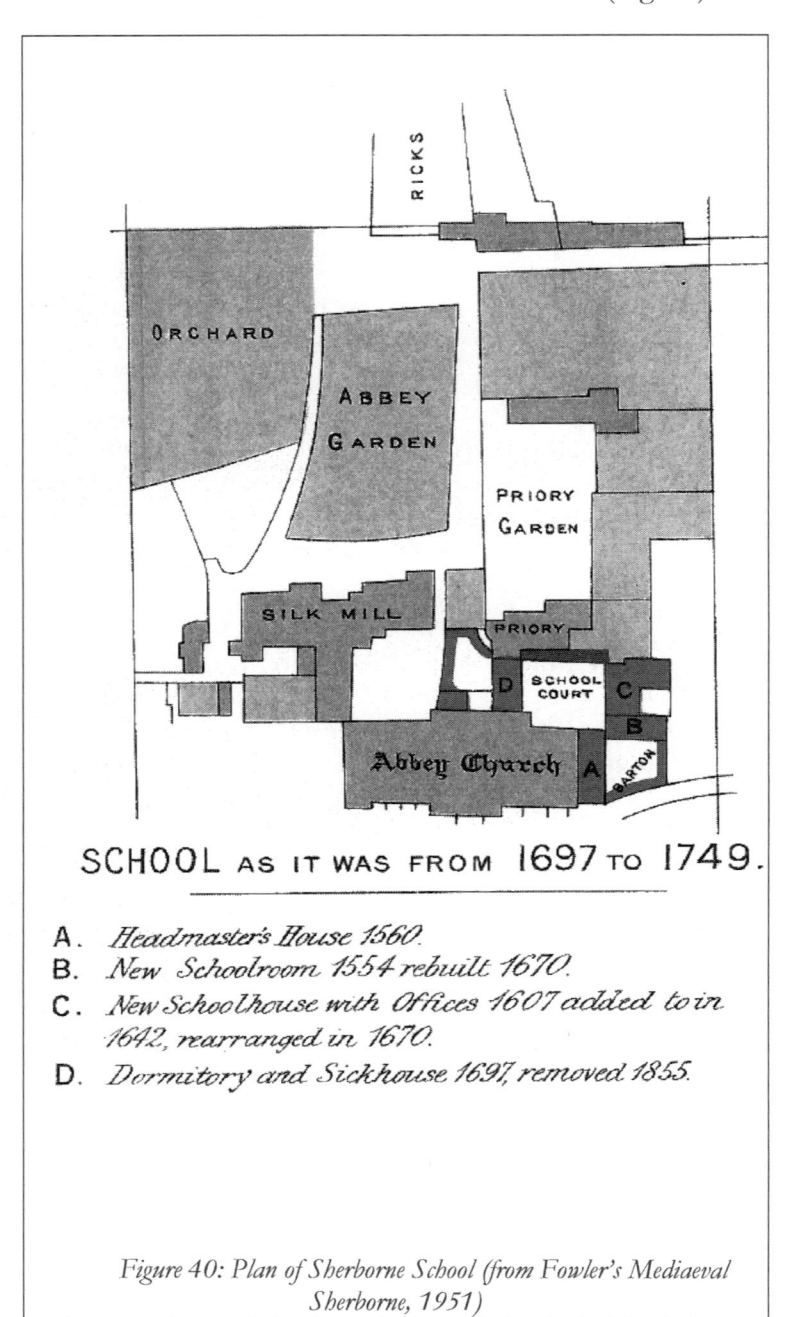

SCHOOL AS IT WAS FROM 1697 TO 1749.

A. *Headmaster's House 1560.*
B. *New Schoolroom 1554 rebuilt 1670.*
C. *New Schoolhouse with Offices 1607 added to in 1642, rearranged in 1670.*
D. *Dormitory and Sickhouse 1697, removed 1855.*

Figure 40: Plan of Sherborne School (from Fowler's Mediaeval Sherborne, 1951)

[2] 1558/79: Chancery Proceedings. Series II bundle 15 of 29. William Rydeowte v Wase & others. [National Archives ref: C3/150/29]

"To Sir Nicholas Bacon, Lord Keeper of the Great Seal of England. William Rydeowte of Sherborne complains that after purchasing from Robert Wase about four years past freehold Lands Tenements viz. 36 acres arable land called Hyle, 2 closes of Meadow and 5 acres of arable land enclosed commonly called Owt Hyle in Sherborne, he cannot obtain them from Defendant who has granted the land to Ellen Thorne & Robert Thorne her brother. William Rydeowte cannot obtain the Deeds of the property & seeks help from the court."

Figure 41: Sir Nicholas Bacon

During this period of history an individual wishing to make a legal case against another, for which common law was thought to be insufficient to mete out justice, employed a lawyer to draw up a bill of complaint setting out the alleged offences and asking the Lord Chancellor to deal with the case. The Rydeowte v Wase documents (the complaint and defence statement) are undated but were addressed to Sir Nicholas Bacon, Lord Keeper of the Great Seal of England (Fig. 41), a position he held between 1558 and 1579. As William had said that he purchased land from Wase "four years past" the transaction could have occurred at any point between 1554 and 1575. Interestingly, Robert Wase was a governor of Sherborne School in 1560 and 1564-1565 and may have been well known to William. This is the first documentary reference to a member of the Ridout family in connection with any part of the Hyle estate.

[3] 1570: William Rydowte, governor of Sherborne School. 'Sherborne Register 1823-1900', published in 1900 by House, H.H. & Rogerson, T.C. Additionally, William was shown as being the warden of the school in 1574.

[4] 1574-1575: Accounts roll for William Rydowte, Warden (& Receiver) Sherborne School [Ref: S235/B1/15].

Figure 42: William Rydowte's account roll for Sherborne School 1574-5

Each year, the gentleman appointed as warden of the school would keep the accounts on a roll of parchment, recording the various expenses relating to the running of the school and income from leases and grants. The script, although lovely to look at, was very hard to read. This is possibly William's own hand or it may have been that of a clerk (Fig. 42).

[5] 1575: 26th September - Lease between 'William Rydeowte and other people of Sherborne and governors (of Sherborne School) and Lawrence Bishop'. [Ref: S235/D1/1/2].

This lease concerned various shops that Bishop had built (and which were physically attached to the schoolhouse). William was named at the head of a wider group of people from Sherborne, perhaps in his capacity as the warden of Sherborne School that year. Lawrence Bishop had been a master of the almshouse in 1560-61, 1562-63 and 1571-72.

[6] 1578-1579: Sherborne Almshouse accounts; William Ridout, Almshouse Master. [Ref: D/SHA/A119] (Fig. 43).

Figure 43: William Ridout's account roll for Sherborne Almshouse, 1578

This is almost certainly the same William Ridout/Rydowte/Rydout as the school Warden in the year 1574-75. The name variation suggests that he was not the writer of this account, or perhaps of the previous one.

Sherborne Almshouse was first established in the fifteenth century, or maybe even before according to some accounts, providing a home to a small number of poor, elderly Sherborne residents. As with the grammar school, upstanding men of the town took it in turns to take charge of the house; some men held the post for two or three years or repeated a year's term at different times. The role of the Almshouse Master included drawing up an account roll, reflecting the year's expenses and the income from a considerable number of local properties owned by the almshouse, the largest of which was Hyle Farm, acquired in ~1440.

[7] 1603: William Rideowte wrote his will on the 1st October:

"The first day of October 1603 I William Rideowte of Chettle in the Countie of Dorset gentleman sick of bodie but of good and pfecte memorie (god be praised) doe make and ordaine this my last will and Testament in manner and forme following That is to say first I commend my Soule into the handes of my maker, hoping assuredly through the merrite of Jesus Christe my saviour to be made partaker of life everlasting And I commend my body to

the earth whereof it was made And to be buried in the parish church of Chettle. Item I give to the repairacon of the said church six shillings eight pence Item I give the church of Sherborne ten shillings Item I give to the Almes house men and women of Sherborne aforesaid four pence apice to every one of them Item I give to Dorothy Rydeowt my servant fourtie shillings [£2.0s.0d] Item I give to William Rydeowte her brother five marks of lawfull English money [£3.6s.8d] Item I give to my wife Alice oute of my lande at Sherborne Thirtie pounds a yeare quarterly to be payed during her naturall life, And conveniente howseroome And the Parlor to her own use in my dwelling house in Chettle, as longe as she liveth Condicionally That upon reasonable request she doe release and relinquish her Dower and all her right and Tytle which she may have or claime of in and to my landes and tenements in Sherborne aforesaide or in any part thereof, or otherwise the said Annuity of Thirtie pounds a yeare to surcease and to be of no force to all intente and purpose Item I give and bequeath to William Rydeowte sonne of Walter Rydeowte my nephew and to the heires male of his body lawfully begotten and to be begotten, All my landes and tenements Rente reversions Service and hereditamentes whatsoever in Sherborne aforesaid or else where unconveyed and not assured unto the said Walter Rydeowte his ffather And for default of such issue, To the said Walter Rydeowte and his heires males of his bodye lawfully begotten and to be begotten And for default of such issue to William Rydeowt sonne of George Rydeowt of Bayford in the County of Somerset [nr. Wincanton, ~17 miles from Sherborne] and to the heires male of his bodye lawfully begotten and to be begotten And for default of such issue to the right heires of William Rydeowt for ever, Provided always that my intent and meaning is That the said Walter Rydeowte shall have the benefit sole and imployment of the saide landes and tenements with their appurtenances untill the saide William Rydeowte his sonne accomplish the age of twenty and fower yeares, And that the said Walter shall keep the said William his Sonne to Schoole, and give him sufficient maintenance to keepe him at Oxforde, and the Innes of Courte, Item I give to William Rydeowte Sonne of Walter Rydeowte my best silver Saltcellar, duble guilt, And my Silver cup of the newe fashion [Jacobean rather than Elizabethan] p..ll Gilt. Item I give to the said William Rideout sonne of the said Walter Rydeowt the Lease of my ffarme in Chettle and all my right and interest thereof withal the terme of yeares thereof yet to come and unexpired Conditionally that the said Walter Rydeowt shall have the use and benefit of the said farme until the said William his sonne shall accomplish the age of twentie foure yeares, And upon Condicion that the said William be ruled by his parents and friendes in all things that shall be for his good otherwise my meaning is That the said Walter Rideout his father shall enjoy it during my whole terme yet to come, And if the said William happen to die before the said Walter his ffather Then the said ffarme to remaine wholie to the said Walter Rydeowte. The residue of all my landes goodes and chattels nott herein before given and bequeathed I doe give and bequeath the same and every of them to the said Walter Rydeowt my nephew whom I make my full and whole Executor of this my last Will and testament and of all my goodes moveable and unmoveable, And I do hereby revoke all former and other will and wills whatsoever by me made, And I doe give to the Preacher that shall speake at my ffunerall six shillings eight pense, And doe constitute and appoint my loving friends George W..dale and Henry Lye gentlemen to be the Overseers of this my last will and testament, praying them to be ayding and assisting to my said Executor, And I doe give them for their paines tenn Shilling apiece."

Witness hereunto Nicholas West and Thomas West Junior. Proved 9th February 1603/4

Figure 44: St Mary's, Chettle. Photo © Nigel Freeman

William Ridowte, gent, was buried on the 14th December 1603 in the churchyard of St Mary's, Chettle (Fig. 44). I found the following were the only other entries for Ridowte, or any name variant, in the Chettle parish registers:

- 14th March 1598: Thomas, the sonne of Thomas Ridowte was christened
- 21st November 1603: Thomas, son of Thomas was buried
- 19th September 1603: Robert Wattes married Dorothie Ridowte

What is very interesting is that William mentioned his servant Dorothy and her brother William and gave each of them a quite generous amount of money. Since I have seen similar examples, I wondered if this undoubtedly wealthy man had employed a poorer family member. It is just possible that Dorothy's brother William is William Ridout of Hyle and Sherborne (1554-1621) and there is one very good reason why this might be so. The parish records for Chettle show that a Dorothy Rideowt married Robert Wattes a few days before William wrote his will - although he still calls her 'Rydeowte' rather than 'Wattes' - could this be William's servant, or perhaps her daughter of the same name? What is the likelihood of there being two unrelated women of this name in a small village at the same time? Seventy-four years later, in the 1677 Sherborne Manor Survey, 58yr old Robert Watts is the copyhold tenant of 'a cottage barne and backside containing halfe an acre formerly Ridouts'. The plot has one and a half acres of pasture at a rent of 2s 4d. According to a 1614 Sherborne Survey, William Ridout (of Hyle) aged 60 and his two sons William and Thomas occupied a copyhold tenement in Nethercombe, identically described as comprising 'one cottage, a barne, garden & backside containing one acre at a rent of 2s 4d. Was Robert Watts (b. ~1619) related to Robert Watts and Dorothy Ridout, or is this just a coincidence? It is an intriguing hypothesis but one which I might never prove. If I am right however, William of Chettle may prove to be part of the Sherborne Ridout family.

Ten years after his death, in 1613, an Inquisition Post Mortem (InqPM) was held regarding William Rydeowte and his estate. An InqPM was an inquiry, undertaken after the death of a feudal tenant-in-chief (a direct tenant of the crown), to establish what lands he held and who should succeed to them. If more than a year had passed since the death of the subject, a *writ of mandamus* was issued to the local escheator, an official responsible for looking after the crown's interests, who would then convene a local jury and conduct the inquiry. If any of the tenant-in-chief's real estate was not settled on friends or family members then it could be taken back by the crown. To avoid this, most tenants-in-chief, perhaps with the help of a good attorney, would convey lands and tenements to trustees that all loose ends were tied up and the estate would pass to the subject's chosen benefactors, not to the crown!

William Rydeowte was probably a wealthy gentleman; he held the leases of several properties and lands in Sherborne, Oborne and Chettle (a village six miles NE of Blandford Forum and about twenty-six miles east of Sherborne). Whilst at his death in 1603 he probably lived on his farm in the village, it is apparent from his numerous appearances in the Sherborne records that, earlier in his life, William was closely involved with the town as it emerged from the turbulent times under Henry VIII.

Here follows a transcript of part of the InqPM (translated from the Latin) which I studied at the National Archives at Kew. I have added comments in square brackets in an attempt to explain the complex content:

Chancery series 10 James I (1613) PRO pt 2 114 William Rydowt, Dorset

"Inquisition indented taken at Shaston [Shaftesbury] in county Dorset in 2nd September 10 James D G of England, France & Ireland & 46 of Scotland Before William Swanston junior Eschoetor on oath of John Boden of the said Lord the King by virtue of a writ of mandamus of the said Lord King that the Eschoetor should make the enquiry.

To enquire after the death of William Ridout gent deceased by the Oath of John Davidge Gent., Walter Ridout, Richard Coombe, Ambrose Burlton, Richard Rives, William Stile, William Cooke, William Swetman, Nicholas Aprichard, Robert Seymer, Thomas Haswell, William Muncton, John Williams, Robert Evered, gent, George Cross, John Hirden honest & lawful men; who say that William Ridout at the time of his death was seized in his demesne in fee tail [William died possessing freehold property that had been granted to him, perhaps by the sovereign, which was only heritable by William's own descendants, of which there were none] of & in 19 messuages one garden & 19 yards in Sherborne & Castleton in tenure & occupation of Richard Orreng, Richard Paynter, William Ridout, John Lambert, Thomas Glune, Robert Bradford, Marjerie Bushrode, Robert Roe, George Garrett, Henry Barnard, John Moone, Henry Bawler, Tristram Turk, William Sampson, Christopher Richman, Paul Hityard [?Hilyard], Bartholomew Ould, David Easterman and Richard Donham…

Either assigned [transferred] or to be assigned divers lands tenements & hereditaments situated in Sherborne Newland & Castleton [Newland and Castletown are both now suburbs of Sherborne] messuages or respective belonging or pertaining & of & in one pasture in Castleton called Magdalen Acre in occupation of [possessed by] Richard Masters or his assigns [persons to whom Masters was free to pass on the property] one other pasture situated in Castleton called Elexarer Close and of & in on other pasture in Sherborne called Outhill containing by estimation 2 acres more or less in the tenure and occupation of Lawrence Mitchell & his assigns and of & in 5 acres of Arable land called Mousehill in fields of Sherborne in manner of tenure & occupation of Robert Foster or his assigns and of & in one close and pasture called Hammonde Meade in Sherborne ffour Yeare tenure and occupation of John Lambert or his assigns and of & in one other pasture called Fower pitts in Sherborne by estimation 4 acres in tenure and occupation of Adam Taylor or his assigns and of & in one pasture called Great Hile containing by estimation XII acres and in one called Hile Mead in Sherborne for William Ridout in Com'n or his assigns and of & in one pasture called Hile in Sherborne lying in Westbridge [Westbury] in tenure & occupation of William Ridout in Com'n ['in commission' meaning the William Rydeowte subject of this InqPM] and of & in one other Pasture in Sherborne in tenure & occupation of William Ridout in Com'n and of & in other pasture called Vertnam in Oborne County Dorset.

On 18th October 43 year of Elizabeth [1601] he settled [splitting the legal and beneficiary aspects of property such that legally William's lands were legally held in trust but he was still the beneficiary i.e. 'user' of them] above lands on William Swanston of Wincanton, John Boden, Thomas Swetman, John Ffowell gent for William Ridouts own use and to the use of Walter Ridout his nephew [translated from original 'nepos'] failing him for the use of Thomazine his wife & heir male Walter aforesaid & Thomazine and to the use of Grace Ridout the eldest daughter of Walter & Thomazine Ridout and after Graces death to the use of the second daughter Ffrancisca & then to Barbara Ridout the third daughter & then to Magdalene the fourth daughter & after her death to heirs male of Walter & Thomazine & failing heirs male to heirs female of the said Walter & Thomazine Ridout failing whom to William son of Robert Ridout of Fontmell & his heirs male born or to be born failing him to Richard another son of aforesaid Robert & his heirs failing him to William son of George Ridout of Wincanton county Somerset lately deceased and his heirs male born or to be born, failing him to aforesaid Robert and his heirs of William aforesaid."

This document shows that William Rydeowte 'of Chettle' held tenure of three pieces of land relating to the Hyle estate (presumably owned by the Almshouse) described as Great Hyle, Hyle Mead and Hyle. In 1620, William Ridout 'of Hyle' bequeathed his 'lease of Hyle' to his son William but with no details of quite how much land was involved; it is hard to imagine that there was no connection between the two Williams.

20. Walter Rydowte of Folke (1564-1643): gentleman & rebel

From all the documentary evidence about William Rydeowte of Chettle, it has been established that Walter Rydeowte was William's nephew and was first mentioned in his uncle's will of 1603 as the beneficiary of estates in Sherborne. As with William, there are several instances where Walter appears in Sherborne records and others:

[1] The Sherborne School Register 1823-1900. Rogerson, TC (1900): From the General List of Shiburnians (p. 294):

"Circ 1575. Rideout, Walter, of Sherborne. BNC Oxon 1580 Governor 1605, Warden 1611."

This entry shows that Walter entered Sherborne School as a pupil in about 1575 and returned several years later, after leaving Oxford University, to become a governor and a warden (see below)

[2] Alumni Oxoniensis 1500-1886, Joseph Foster:

'Ridout, Walter, of Dorset, pleb. Brasenose College., matric entry under date 18 July 1580 aged 16.'

The word pleb., short for plebeian in this context, means that Walter was regarded as a commoner rather than as a son of gentry or an aristocrat. Obviously, if he matriculated (registered) in 1580 at the age of sixteen, this means that he was probably born in ~1564 and entered Sherborne School when he was eleven.

[3] Declaration of Trust between (a) The Governors of Sherborne School and (b) Laurence Swetnam, gent, John Foster, Walter Rydowte, gent and Robert Whetcombe all of Sherborne. Property: The School House, from (a) to (b) on condition: that (b) holds the property in trust for the remainder of the lease for the use of the Grammar School. 27th August 1605 [Ref: S235/D1/1/3]

These gentlemen were all governors of the School at this point; the document shows that they jointly shared a role as trustees for the building, which was used by the School.

[4] Sherborne Almshouse, account of Walter Rydowte, Master (1608-09) [Ref: D/SHA/A177 & 178]. See the similar entry for William.

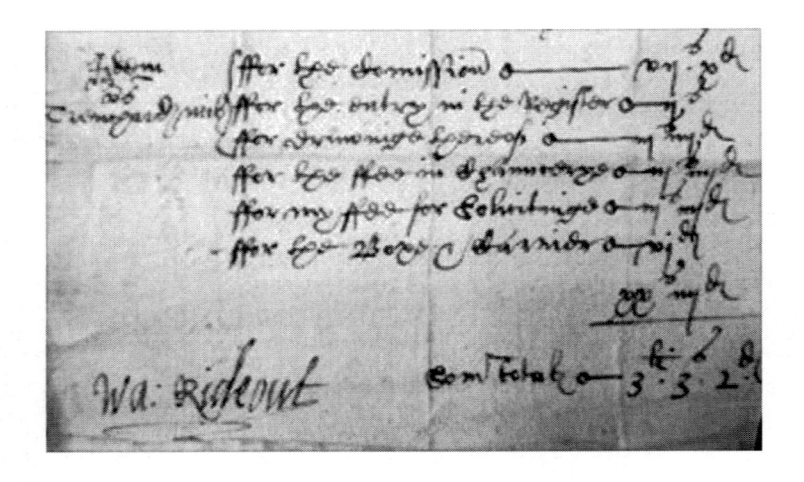

Figure 45: Walter Rideout's school accounts, 1611

[5] Sherborne School, Walter Rydout, collector for certain shambles (1610-11) [Ref: S235/C5/2/23]

Shambles (sometimes written as 'shammells') were small market stalls, selling fish or meat, many of which were leased and operated by the governors of Sherborne School. These stalls were owned by the school to which the leaseholders paid rent providing another source of income to the establishment. Walter, as warden of the school, was collecting these rents and keeping accounts; illustrated appears to be a list of his expenses (Fig. 45)

[6] Sherborne School. Draft Account for Walter Rydowte (1611-12) [Ref: S235/B1/52/1]. See the similar entry for William.

[7] Sherborne Manor Survey 1614.

Walter held 'diverse houses and lands' as a freeholder (ownership in perpetuity rather than by a lease) in 'Sherborne Manor' (rent 14s 8d), 'Castleton' (£5 0s 4d) and a dovecote at Barton Farm let to William Fisher. His service was by swearing fealty, presumably to the Lord of the Manor. These properties probably represent those bequeathed to him by his uncle, William of Chettle in 1603.

[8] Chancery case, 19 James I. Ridout v Standen, 7th February 1623

"Walter Ridout the Orator of Alweston Gent. Whereas Edward Standen of Sherborne yeoman about 4th year of Elizabeth (1562) obtained a decree in Chancery against John Meere and William Meere of Sherborne, gentlemen of and concerning three tenements in Sherborne: Standen pressed for the money and said Meere mortgaged the three tenements to John Starr of Yeovil, Dorset for 100 marks and for non-payment Standen "bussed" a forfeiture to said Joseph Starr in .... and that the said John & William Starr had notice of the same etc. etc. Standen being then a stranger to Walter Ridout made means by his brother-in-law Walter Ffryer to obtain access to him and Walter Ridout lent him the money to redeem the tenements from Starr: they continued to importune your orator and his wife till the money was lent. "He could have no rest for her weepeinge". Thereon about two years past your Orator lent Standen £65 to redeem the tenements on which Standen assigned the three tenements to the Orator for the rest of his term. Six months since failing payment, your Orator became possessed of them absolutely. John Meere then sent a letter to your Orator (one clothier & Henry Meere mentioned) and by & bye your Orator entered upon the tenements upon which " Johan ye wife of ye said Standen tooke a long rise out of ye hedge and sette upon your Orator threwe stones at him. Wherewith her boye sett a greate Mastiffe dogge att your Orator in so much yet if your Orator having then but a Cudgell in his hand not well defended himselfe from ye said Mastiffe he had torne out his throate". John Ffoster of Sherborne, yeoman persuaded Thomasine Starr a young girl to be a partner for the payment of the money. These troubles have been going on for the Orator seven years before that suit and eight years since. In all fifteen years. Your Orator being an Attorney-at-law was persuaded to sue John Oke of Sherborne yeoman – mentions also John Ffawkener gent & Robert Colbery Attorney."

This document shows that, apart from having had a rather difficult time with an irate woman and her dog, Walter was an attorney, presumably having studied law at Oxford and, as it transpires, at the Inns of Court (see p.131). It also suggests that Walter may have married a female with the maiden name of Fryer. There are other chancery proceedings which give small clues to family events, for example the case of Ridout v Vincent. (1624) in which Joan Vincent, sister of Walter Ridout, is mentioned and Ridout v Whetcombe (1627) records that Walter's daughter Barbara was married to Thomas Whetcombe but had died in 1625 (see burial record: 8th September 1625 at Folke, 'Barbara Whetcomb, uxor Thome Whetcomb, sept.'). Ridout v Keynes (1631) says that, at the time of a prospective sale, Walter was busy 'about a marriage of his eldest son'. Walter's son William lost his first wife, Mary FAUNTLEROY after the birth of a daughter Dorothy, baptised on the 21st April 1630; Mary was buried eight days later at Folke; see also administration of the estate of Mary Rideout alias Ffauntleroy granted 20th November 1630 to William Rideout of Alweston, Dorset, husband. At some point, William married Ann BALLARD from Lamberhurst in Surrey, a wedding that may have taken place in 1631, although I can find no documentary evidence for it.

[8] The Almshouse of SS John, Sherborne guide book (p.6): 'A brother committing an offence was fined.

In 1637 Walter Ridout, when ordered to pay a certain sum of money spake many undecent and high words… amongst other words hee sayd Mr Hele of Clifton Maybank had never a hound of a bigger mouth than the Steward Mr Wright had!' Clearly, Walter was sometimes a bit outspoken; at this point, he was about 75 years old.

[9] Sherborne School: Statement issued by Walter Ridout protesting against the expulsion order by the Governors, because of his support for the Roundheads (1642). [Ref: S235/A2/5/2].

This document, written in Walter's small and meticulous hand, is his response to the threat of expulsion from the Brotherhood of Sherborne Almshouse but sadly he was expelled shortly thereafter. It seems from what I have read that the 'powers that be' considered Walter too cantankerous (or possibly too honest) and seized an opportunity to be rid of him but Walter was an attorney and fought his corner by counter accusations of corruption and nepotism against the town's elders. Strangely though, he did not offer a rebuttal of the allegations made against him, point out his long years of service or even ask for Christian charity and forgiveness. The statement may be read at the end of this chapter.

On the south wall inside St Lawrence's church in Folke is a monument to Walter; it is a tablet with an arched panel and once bore painted emblems of immortality (Fig. 46). His age at death in 1643 was said to be 84 yrs, which is either wrong, or means that Walter was born ~1559 and went up to Oxford unfashionably late at the age of twenty-one. The inscription, now badly worn, reads:

An Epitaph on Walter Rideout Gentleman Which he himself made A little before His decease. He dyed the 22 day of October at age of four score and four Anno Dom 1643.
Here lyeth a true christian now at quiet rest
Who whilst he lived was by ye world oprest
But praysed be God he overcame this evill
And vanquished hath ye world ye flesh and devil

Figure 46: Walter's epitaph in Folke Church

Walter may have been a 'pleb' when he entered Oxford University but was recorded as 'generosus' or 'gentleman' by 1609, possibly as a result of inheriting property from his uncle William. It is self evident that at some point before his death, Walter and his wife moved from Cann to Sherborne and then to Folke, although he was involved with business in Sherborne throughout.

The 'Members of Oriel College, Oxford' (Registrum orielense, book 1, p. 165) shows an entry which reads simply 'Rideout (Riddut) admitted commoner 1618-1619' with no indication of forename or other details. A commoner is defined as a student who does not have a scholarship. The 'usual' age of entry at university in the 17th century was about 16 suggesting that 'Rideout' was born in about 1601/2. Could this be William, son of Walter whose education was provided for by William of Chettle's will?

From all the documents above and parish records, here is the descendancy from Walter:

Walter of Allweston (Folke), gentleman, born 1564. 'Mr Walter Rideout (who died at Caundle Marsh) was buried the 27th October 1643 at ffolke church'; attorney. Walter married Thomazine (?)Fryer, who was buried at Folke: 'Tamsam, the widow of Mr Walter Ridout deceased was buried the 4th day of September 1657'. The couple had several children:

1. Grace (no baptism found) married at Sherborne 17th April 1615 to Leonard NOX
2. Frances(ca) bp. Cann, 20th October 1594, daughter of Walter, bur. 31st October 1607 in Sherborne
3. Barbara bp. Sherborne 16th July 1596; died 1625; married at Sherborne 1st June 1618 to Thomas WHETCOMBE of Folke
4. Magdaline bp. Sherborne 4th February 1598/59
5. William of Allweston bp. 13th Dec 1601 in Sherborne; bur. Folke 1st July 1671. Married Mary, daughter of William FAUNTLEROY of Fauntleroy's Marsh, bur. Folke on the 29th April 1630; they had a daughter:
    5.1 Dorothy, bp. Folke 21st April 1630
William married secondly Ann BALLARD of Lamberhurst Sussex and had:-
    5.2 Anne, bp. Folke 16th November 1638, bur. Mayfield 17th August 1699
    5.3 Margaret, bp. Folke 1st Nov 1639, bur. Folke on the 15th November 1641
    5.4 William, bp. Folke 29th December 1641. He inherited a house & land at Lamberhurst from his Uncle Richard Ballard
    5.5 Richard, bp. Folke 4th September 1644, bur. Mayfield 14th July 1694. Married Sarah DOBELL on the 18th Dec 1684
    5.6 John bp. Folke 30th May 1646, bur. Folke 30th May 1667
    5.7 Mary bp. Folke 19th June 1650, bur. Uckfield 18th September 1688. Married Gabriel EAGLES

    5.8 Walter bp. Folke 12th September 1652. Lived in Wiltshire; died before 1695.
    5.9 Helina bur. Folke 7th July 1661.
6. Alse bp. Sherborne 22nd December 1606 'daughter of Walter'
7. Margaret bp. 9th April 1609, daughter of Walter generosus
8. Walter bp. 23rd June 1611, bur. 6th July 1615, son of Walter generosus
9. John bp. 29th May 1614, son of Walter generosus

The first five of Walter's children were named in William Rydeowte of Chettle's InqPM in order of seniority, confirmed by parish records, and the terms of William's will. Walter's younger children, of course, had not been born in William's lifetime. Today there may still be living descendants of this family who can claim one of Walter's sons as their ancestor and, although I am sure that this wasn't the easiest of men to like, I would be happy to claim him as a family member.

Walter Ridout's statement to Sherborne Almshouse - 1642

It has taken a colleague and fellow family historian, Prof. John Templeton (to whom my grateful thanks), and myself several weeks to fully transcribe and make sense of this long and rambling letter. It was written on the 24th June 1642 by Walter Ridout in protest to his proposed expulsion from the Brotherhood of Sherborne Almshouse, allegedly for having Roundhead sympathies. In the early days of the English Civil War, most of the country was more inclined to remain neutral but clearly the Brothers of the Sherborne Almshouse considered themselves loyal to the Crown; nonetheless, removing a fellow Brother in such peremptory fashion does seem exceedingly harsh. At this point, Walter was seventy-eight years old and had joined the Brethren in 1609.

This document was quite hard to read; in his small, legal hand, Walter had crammed nearly four thousand words onto two sides of foolscap parchment. Some words remain undecipherable, hence the occasional gaps, and their meaning can be difficult to equate with our modern way of talking. However, it is clear that Walter was an accomplished attorney and had an argument for every point with which he had been charged by the other Brothers. He seems to have held grudges against many others in the governing body of the Almshouse (and School) and railed against elders who had long since died. Walter sounds like a man of high moral principles who believed that many of his peers were corrupt; he no doubt saw their condemnation of him as unjust and hypocritical. Walter's appeal was, not surprisingly considering that the case was judged by those whom he had spoken against, turned down and, at the bottom of the document is a sentence suggesting that he was ejected from the Brotherhood not long after the statement was made.

The words in square brackets are my own; those in rounded brackets belong to Walter. I have 'Anglicised' the translation a little in order for it to make any sense at all; the original language is archaic, having been written 371 years ago. This record is of general historical interest, because Walter is 'speaking' in his own words; it is a personal statement and tells us something about his life in the small rural town of Sherborne during the mid 16th century, just as the Civil War was starting. On a family history level, Walter reveals certain interesting facts, for example that his father had lived in Shillingstone (does 'living' imply that he had been a rector?) and that he himself had been granted Arms by a herald's visitation at some point.

The answer of Walter Ridout to the unjust, unequal and unchristian-like orders of the master and brethren of the Almshouse of Sherborne.

"The said Walter Ridout says that the orders which they have made against him are most scandalous, wicked and unjust having no ground, neither from God's law nor man's law, but set by the odious malice of some ancients of the company who, standing upon their antiquity, turn the laws and statutes of the house into iniquity. And to strengthen their position have chosen theirs sons and now their wives and daughters begin to come after for they take their place here of late, at the Account, which was not allowed in former times. And send about meat to some of the master's wives and some other religious people being a ... to others of the company who are as worthy of it as the best of them.

Mr Lyford and some others of the company may remember how Mistress Cooth at the Account taxed me at the table for being quarrelsome with her husband; not so quarrelsome as he was with me when he laid violent hands upon me. His wife, you see, begins to talk, but women must talk at home and not in the church nor in the Almshouse.

Can you find any such precedent in the [Alms]house that a young upstart, as young Chetmill is, being then Master should such person to make an order and to set a fine upon his ancient head for speaking indecent words, which are not expressed in the order, which none that have judgement or true understanding would have given way to? But being charged again and again by this young master with the steward; will you do nothing, my masters, will you do nothing? And being prompted by his malicious father and seconded by an unjust steward Wright, by his cousin Cooth, cousin Whetcombe and cousin Speed, for he would be cousin to anybody who made an order against me, such an order .... had any judgement or understanding would have been to have had a hand in it.

And what was this order for? For saying a spade is a spade, for saying old Wright would out-row any hound [Sir John] Hele [of Clifton Maybank] had, which I do not deny. Do not all know that he did row me out from the upper end of the room even to the door with indecent cries "send for Mr Lyford, send for Mr Lyford" [William Lyford was Vicar of Sherborne]. "Mr Ridout, you did none so disgrace yourself in your life" which many other disgraceful words which I did hear. And cannot I justify my words? Think none are worse than hounds, worse than horses, worse than dogs, worse than asses? See the first [chapter] of Isaiah [verse] 3: "The ox knows his owner and the ass his master's crib, but Israel hath not known me". See David's psalm: "in diverse places where men are counted worse than dogs, worse than hounds for they sin against more knowledge"

But old brother Cooth did slanderously charge me that I did call old Wright 'dog' which I deny, for I make a great difference between a hound and Mr Cooth's mastiff dog for a hound is more genteel and contented compared to a hound for his scent. And therefore he may be more fittingly compared to a hound for his scent, for he took such a scent of my Lord Bristol's good diet that they could not tell how to be rid of him for he would eat as much as two men!

But this 'roarer' was not so content but I, standing at my door the Saturday after, he came by and could not but tell me there were twelve had confirmed the order against me and not one of them spoke a word for me. Now of these twelve, I challenge most of them and first I challenge Richard Speed, that Hotspur [rash and impetuous person], for he has been, if he is not now, a great usurer [lender of money at inflated interest] and has not made restitution to Nathaniel Daniell, whose children cry out against him for a mortgage he took of their father's mill for £60 for half a year; and would not lend his money longer unless Daniell would pull out one of his children [remove him as a life on a tenancy] and put one of Speed's into the lease. Therefore let him stand by for his voice is worth nothing.

For by the canon law a usurer ought not to come into the congregation but stand as an excommunicated person; he ought not to bear testimony in any cause; he ought not to make a will, for his goods be not his own; he ought not to be buried in Christian burial but in the highway and by the old law he is held worse than a thief for a thief was to restore double but the usurer was to restore fourfold. The sin is not forgiven without restitution.

I challenge also on old brother Cooth and brother Whetcombe for the like, for they take up wares from London and other places upon usury for five months and make the country people treble and quadruple their usury [interest]. I may also challenge Mr Cooth, who has lost his place, being out of the town alone a year and day, while his whole family are not coming to do the house any service, who by the Charter is to be put out and to house another. In the like case is Jonathan Penny and, contrary to the others, you suffer them to continue in their place. In the like case is Mr Compton.

I challenge old brother Chetmill for foul extortion and cheating the three hatters of ? Crakehorn [illegible] and for usury to Mr Bart of Wootton who though he be dead, yet the sin remains by an annuity of £40 a year to be paid to his children. His alms deed cannot help it, for restitution must be made to the party wronged and how the sin can be forgiven, the sin remaining; it is a hard task. For this is worse than thievery, for the thief dying the sin dies with him but we see here the sin remains after the usurer is dead by an annuity or bond or both, which is a fearful case.

But the usurers say the borrower is as bad as the lender, taking hold of Mr Lyford's speech, not long said in the pulpit, where he said, as it is in the 24 of Isaiah [24:2] "like people like priest, like maid like mistress, like buyer like seller, like lender like borrower upon usury". The prophet, these conclude under sin, he says not that the borrower is as bad the lender for it is lawful to borrow as on 'Sermon' Christ says "from him that doth borrow turn not away thy face". But it is unlawful to lend upon usury.

I also challenge old Wright, though he be dead, too for he was out of the town 30 years, and never came to do any service. And for a fighter in my Lord's Court I ….. and contrary to the Charter you took him in again whereas you should have chosen another in his place. And herein you have broken the fundamental laws and statute of the house, which should maintain the body of the Corporation and therein have forsworn yourselves with … worst of all. Now there is no full jury therefore your orders are void and though Jonathan Penny one of the company, who hath also lost his place, told me that these orders would remain against me of record forever yet. I will not give him a halfpenny to blot them out for it will be more to the shame of them that made them than me. But I have more against those malicious adversaries and cannot … them so look into the [verse] 1 of the Cor[inthians] 5; there you shall find that if any is called a brother be a fornicator, or an idolator, or a reviler, or a drunkard, or an extortioner nor keep him company. I need not go about to prove it; you all know it is as well as I and the whole town and county to the odious covetousness of our brother Cooth and brother Whetcombe that cannot suffer their neighbours to live by them in their trade but they take it away from them. And what odious darkness is and has been in their shops these 30 or 40 years which God and the world. Covertness is idolatry, worse than drunkenness.

But I have heard some preachers say it is a devilish thing to reprove others, having no calling to do it. I think it is more devilish in them that have a calling to reprove it and do wink at it and seek no remedy for such a … sin. And yet I will tell you I have a calling to do it and as good a calling as any hath as will deny it which I will not exchange for any calling under heaven and that is the calling of a Christian which no man of judgement will deny to be the best calling of all callings. I will not change it to be a justice of the peace.

I have some what also against Mr Lyford who is apt to receive … report against me, as when he sent his bell man Nott to me for a coffin, which I bought of the churchwardens for 35 years ago and he, without examining the matter, sent for the coffin for it was a church good giving credence unto some religious slanders …. wherein he wronged me to give rash judgment against me before he had heard my answer. And further he confirmed an order which the wife Masters made against me (why those words) "if no order will bind him let the order stand" had Mr …. made me so disorderly thus to condemn me before a trial upon report of malicious adversaries. Herein he shows his weakness, though a learned clerk. According to that saying 'the greatest clerk be not the wisest man' from when heretofore I taxed him for it, that it was a great sin to receive false tales, he told me he must believe as three or four must believe one which I …?dente for vox populi [the voice of the people] is no Diaboli [devil] for it condemned Christ and delivered Barrabas see Exodus 23: "Thou shalt not follow a multitude to doe evil: neither shalt thou speak in a cause, to decline after many, to wrest judgement".

In old times, no sentence passed against any man but upon testimony of other witnesses besides the accusers for none might be …. witnesses and judge as he and the company are. Do you find this in Scriptures to keep that from me which so long I laid out of my purse for the house. And all you can say against it 'you keep account of it'. You kept me accounted of Mr Lodge four pounds he laid out … ? cow yet you paid him. And therefore your answer to me is very childish and foolish. I do keep account of it and I charge you through William Sansome and others of the company report that I did confess myself satisfied, but not paid. I confess I was satisfied in the coming carriage of the reversion, for Mr Lodge showed me the account. They will by such bear?? But he was i…. by the ancient cunning pleaders before hand what to do. But if I leave you this unless you give me later satisfaction then I will, if God send me life. You have very bound to old Chetmill for business he did for the house and gave him 40 shillings more than his bill of charge came to as appear the extent upon the account, been liberal to Reape one of the religious company, and … night preacher. And gave him eight or ….. pay and …

And now to make a full answer to all your orders and ….. Give me leave, I pray you, to deliver my mind and when I have done, make one for when heretofore I have had speech with you in the house, five or six will talk all together, as if you were in the alehouse, that it is impossible for one man to answer you altogether. And now to answer one, Brother Hodges [and] others for some thing that they have taxed me with for uncharitableness in speaking ill of the dead to the common saying 'nil nisi bona de mortuis' must I be bound by this to speak well of Jezebel, who was a whore and a witch, and of many other wicked ones spoken of in scripture, and say they were good people, when the word of God tells who otherwise I would be glad to learn any good things from them, if they were able to teach me. Sure I am they can teach me to slander.

And they put an action on me' that I am contentious and taxed me with common barratry [persistently stirring up quarrels - in the Courts or out of them] to which I answer that if the master of the house be accounted Beelzebub much more must the servant and if the life of a true Christian by continual warfare as I find it in the Scripture then may I say I would rather wear the badge of a Christian than the badge of a banterer or contentious person for no sooner had God cast an estate upon me, which is near forty years ago [Walter inherited his Uncle William's estate in 1603], the world and the Devil set upon me that I was not in peace since, yet I thank God I stand in defence of them both, holding this ground (that it is no great matter to be firm when there is nothing to shake it) and no sooner out of one trouble but into another, no sooner rid of the moors but vexed with an outstanding monster of unthankfulness (God knows I do not slander him). Then troubles with chasing a forester with many others. And now which one brethren of the Almshouse but from such brethren good Lord deliver us.

But Mr Lyford he tells me that I pluck these troubles upon me. Did Mr Lyford pluck that trouble upon himself when he was like to lose his vicarage? Why did he not sit still and let it alone which, if he might have gone without a vicarage and if it please God to exercise me with too powerful enemies, the world and the devil must not I stand up against them, yes though they be legion, by their own confession. And if they were ten legions I would not fear for I am confident there will be more with me than against me.

Should then neighbours to Brethren rejoice about another man's affliction and add affliction to affliction? That is wicked and devilish; those are miserable comforters. But to come to a point: if you have dealt so unjustly, with me to reject me from your Company, and fine me for indecent words which the Scripture doth warrant. For which of them will you expel me? Expel first your odious covetousness & maliciousness out of your breasts and of the odious darkness in your shops. And let your light so shine before men that they may see your good works. And from then you shall the better see duty towards God and towards your neighbours and until you do that you stand incorrigible. Has Mr Whetcombe been a Grand Jury man these twenty-three years to reform sin? And yet he will darken his shop (which is a ... and against the law) because his cousin Cooth does. Truly, I do believe that if his cousin Cooth kept an alehouse, he would do so too for we see he follows him in all trades and ale has a quick return.

When I had often heretofore demanded my money, old Chetmill told me that the money I had received of Thomas Chetmill must be repaid again for I could not keep one for another. I kept it in my hand in the old master's time & since nearly twenty years and yet you pluck it out of my hand most basely and to stop my mouth, old Chetmill told me I was a common barrator, which was most false. And old Wright called me so again & again, which you know I have recused [challenged] to their shame and prove them fools and knaves who persecuted me. Then Josias Cooth told me they would prove it in the blind house; I gave him answer he must put me then into his Shop for I know no other blind house in the town. Then old Brother Cooth laid violent hands upon me to throw me out of the house and once the young master, Chetmill, told me I had deferred the pillory for the business at Blandford Inn for common barratry. Now, if you be not basely partial, why would you not set a fine upon their heads rather than upon mine, for I have not slandered them in any words which I can not prove against them? Mr Lyford set his hand for a petition which Mr Thorne & John Marten put into Parliament yet for ought I see he gives way unto it, otherwise it were an easy matter for him to remedy it for if he cannot name a Brother I cannot tell how he can then name another. I would not for a penny be so faulty for I should preach it in the pulpit, where ministers have the advantage, for we cannot give them an answer, 'til we came in plain ... with them. And there we may talk ... ... what is fitting.

But to come to an end: once young Master Chetmill gave me disgraceful words that I was a thatcher, which I know I ... on this occasion. That when this young gent was Master, I coming into the room, he sitting above all in the window, I saluted all but did not stoop low enough it seems for this young master, for he reprimanded me that I came in very irreverently. Whereupon, at another meeting there I taxed him for it and told him I had been bred at the University and at the Inns of Court and was not now to learn manners from a weaver's loom; herein I hope I spoke nothing in disparagement of the weavers for I hold it an honest calling, but to show him a difference in callings and that the weaver must not go beyond his ground as the expert (Sutor, ne ultra crepidam) ["Shoemaker, not above the sandal", avoid passing judgment beyond your expertise]. And a thatcher is an honest calling, and in truth, a higher calling than a weaver, for he works to know the head and the weaver to cover the tail. I was not bred a thatcher, nor my father neither; he lived at Shillingtone, nine miles off, where his living was well known to be worth a hundred pounds a year and cost him to my uncle £110 or more in my ?bredd. Sir Thomas Freke [1563-1633, MP] was no butcher, though his grandfather was one, [Sir] Nathaniel Napper [1588-1635, MP] was no fishmonger, though his grandfather was one. Can ... Miller, Browne & Williams and many others.

Paul took some reputation unto him that he was a Roman and bred at the feet of Samuel and I may take it some reputation to have been of such breed, though I know reputation to be but another man's breath, which today may extol me and applaud me and tomorrow may vilify and disgrace me. Whose ... may see the pride of this young fellow, his *father but a …… but did weave his … smock, as James Fisher, as others do. And I and others do know he cheated John Fryer of a good Holland shirt [of superior linen] in London, borrowed whilst his rag shirt was a washing and could never have it again. I had a warrant to put him in court but I was loathe to disgrace him. And now, upon his father's tomb, he writes 'gent', which should rather have been 'weaver' or 'maltster' for the herald will not alter it. For he cannot write 'gent' by his practice, for it was foul and full of odious extortion. And he was no sworn attorney for an attorney may write 'gentleman', by the ancient laws of the land, but a solicitor may not.*

He that has five plough lands of inheritance may by the Ancient Law write 'gentleman', which I had and more before I passed it to my sons. And the herald came down in the country many years ago and compelled myself and Thomas Swetnam to take arms [the right to bear a coat of arms]. Heretofore I assume no more than is lawful for we were both bred at the university and at the Inns of Court. But let us leave these fooleries and seek to take our pedigree from Christ for if we could derive it from Noah's Flood yet we may come from cursed Ham as well as blessed Shem: 'ind nobilitis … … virtus', only virtue makes a gentleman. But this young man told me that he would spend I know not what to maintain his father's reputation, which all the county, far and near, do condemn for odious extortion. How should he, with a good conscience … which in these fourteen years was worse than a groat, leave such an estate behind him? If we may conjecture, by uttered things: "the very heavens did shed a Noah's Flood of tears at his burial that there was never seen such a water in that … by no man's time". But we leave the judgement to the searcher of all hearts.

Now to conclude: I have, as I conceive, answered all your observations and therefore do desire your present answer herein, whether you will pay me my money or not, for I will no longer be denied; if I cannot have it in peace, which I have a long time desired, I will get it by other means if I can, as God lends me life. Mr Cooth, being Warden, carried the bag of my four pounds that year; Mr Whetcombe, the next year two hundred pounds; Mr Starr the next year two hundred and twenty pounds. I never got a penny by the house; sure I am [that] I have lost above ten pounds by detaining my money so many years after the suit of usury."

Footnote:

f. "Walter Rideout gentleman is fined 20 nobles for being a barrator [disturber of the peace] is committed until he has paid and until he gives security for his good behaviour for leaving Court without permission. Walter Rideout gentleman is fined 10s for an assault on Abigail, wife of Thomas Devenish." [QS - 323] Blandford 12-15 January 1636 Gaol calendar. Source: Thomas Devenish (c1589 - Aft 1638) Keeper of Dorset Gaol. Research notes compiled by Michael Russell, Online Parish Clerk for Fordington.

21. An investigation of Ridout heraldry

When John Ridout (bp. 1730; see Chapter 9) was chosen to be employed as secretary to Horatio Sharpe, colonial Governor of Maryland, he was 21 years old. The son of George Ridout a miller and baker in Sherborne, John's upbringing had probably been reasonably modest. Neither a pauper nor a gentleman by rank, his father had sent him to Oxford University, which suggests that the boy was particularly bright. Records show that John matriculated as a plebeian (commoner) on the 9th March 1748/49 at Corpus Christi, a college most associated with studies in the humanities. The following extract from Sherborne Almshouse records shows that John was considered a 'poor boy'.

The Sherborne Almshouse Register (Dorset Record Society, 2013; ed. Ann Clark) tells of a charitable bequest made by Dr Nathaniel HIGHMORE, an eminent surgeon, anatomist and physician who practiced in Sherborne for more than forty years. The terms of his 1684 will read: "… I give (that) £5 per annum to such poor boys as shall be sent from the Free Grammar School in Sherborne by the choice of the governors at the school and the master with my executors to the university for the (same) term of six years, if he shall continue there so long, and so from time to time during the term of seventy years." Hence, a deserving student would receive money for up to six years but when he left this gift would be passed to another student. These entries relate to John:

"*4th November 1751: The term of six years is expired during which Samuel Berjew received the £5 yearly pursuant to Dr Highmore's will. It is agreed that John Ridout, son of George Ridout of Sherborne of Corpus Christi College, Oxford, shall have the yearly sum of £5 from the 25th March last past.*

8th June 1753: The above mentioned John Ridout has left the university and has vacated the grant given by Dr Highmore."

After John arrived in America in 1753, according to family lore, he used a Ridout heraldic device, presumably a crest on household items, stationery, or maybe a seal. I don't know how John determined which arms he should use, although there were texts, then as now, and heraldic painters who could be employed. Perhaps the blazon (description) had been passed on by word of mouth through the family, although John's direct ancestor, and mine, was

Figure 47: Arms of Ridout, from Chadwick

William Ridout of Hyle in Sherborne (1554-1621) and there are no records, of which I am aware, that show that this man bore arms of any description or that he descended from an earlier grantee of arms.

As previously discussed, more than one source of Ridout family history has misleadingly stated that John's grandfather, Christopher Ridout was baptised in 1664, or that he was from Henstridge in Somerset, or both. For example, in 'Ontarian Families' by Edward M. Chadwick (Toronto, 1895), from which Figure 47 is taken, the section on Ridouts opens "This is a branch of a family long seated in counties Dorset and Somerset, England of whom Christopher Ridout of Sherborne co. Dorset, baptised 24th Nov 1664, son of Christopher Ridout and Edith his wife, married Mary Glover….". Interestingly, the blazon of these arms is also recorded in 'A Genealogical and Heraldic History of the Colonial Gentry' (Vol. 2, 1895) by Sir Bernard Burke, Ulster King of Arms. The entry specifically related to Percival Frederic Joseph Ridout (b. 1836) of Toronto, 2x great grandson of George Ridout of Sherborne: Arm*s: per pale Ar. and Gu. a Griffin segreant counterchanged* Crest*: A Nag's head coupled ppr Motto: Aquila non capit muscas*" (the eagle does not catch flies). The use of italics, according to Ashworth Peter Burke, editor and son of the author, indicated that the arms, "though actually in use, were borne without authority" and that these were "for the most part assumptions of armorial bearings of families resident in England, Ireland or Scotland, with whom no relationship is proved." In Chadwick, the arms were once again shown in italics, with the same explanation.

Although the family tree illustrated in Sir Bernard Burke's book included John Ridout, Percival Frederic Joseph's x2 great uncle, there was no reference to a prior grant of arms and so, in order to understand why John had taken the used the arms of the griffin, I decided to investigate the subject of heraldry in general, with particular reference to Rid(e)outs. After several months of research I found two lines, carrying very different arms.

Arms: Per pale Argent and Gules a Griffin segreant counterchanged

According to Arthur George Ridout (Ridout book, page 1), arms were confirmed in 9 Henry VIII (1518) to John RIDOEN of Exeter and were, by descent, passed to Thomas Ridout of Henstridge. Arthur described the arms and also a crest (a component of the heraldic display that sits on top of the helmet): 'out of a ducal Coronet Or, a demi Griffin segreant, per pale Argent and Gules. Although a duke's coronet suggests nobility, according to several sources on armoury it was more likely to have been purely decorative. That these arms were confirmed suggests an earlier grant. Variants of Ridoen include Ryden, Rydon, Royden or Roydon.

The earliest mention that I could find of a Ridoen, although not a John, was of Robert Ridoen, or Rydon, 'of the City of Exeter, gentleman, whose ancestors were most inhabited in the county of Devonshire'. He had a grant or confirmation of arms from Clarenceux, King of Arms in 1494 according to Ernest Bland Royden [see: 'Three Royden Families' by E B Royden; pub. Edinburgh 1924]: 'Silver and Gules party per pale, a Gryffon counter of the same with a Gryffon issuing from a crown as crest' The author gave a reference for this grant or confirmation as Harl[h]. MS 1116 folio 37d and added that in Harl. MS 5887 folio 50, there was another reference to the grant but which bore an erroneous date, 9 Hen VIII (1518) rather than the correct 9 Hen VII (1494). It is possible that this error was the source of Arthur's belief in a 1518 grant or confirmation to a John Ridoen or Rydoen, which he mentions twice in his notes although with no source or reference; interestingly, he didn't refer to Robert Ridoen or Rydon or to a 1494 grant. The second folio included an illustration of the arms 'in trick' (Fig. 48), that is a rough monochrome outline in which the tinctures (colours) are replaced by letters i.e. a for argent (silver), g for gules (red) and o for or (gold).

Figure 48: Roydon arms in trick

Robert Rydon was the son of Robert and Marjerie; he became a Notary Public and later the Clerk of the King's Council firstly to Henry VII, then briefly to Henry VIII, moving from Exeter to London in about 1480. Robert's father, also Robert, was an attorney in the King's Court at Westminster; references to him can be found in documents as old as 1450. Mention of 'Master' Robert Rydon (in a legal case) infers that young Robert had studied at Oxford (he was referred to in some documentation as a 'Bachelor in Laws'); his time at university was apparently funded by the rector of St Mary Major in Exeter. Payments made to him in respect of various Commissions carried out in Devon are recorded as having been paid by the City of Exeter and he was eventually awarded a pension from the city in 1502. Robert left a will, dated 19th July 1503 (probate 20th November 1509) in which he requested that his feoffees (trustees) raise sufficient funds from his estate to pay for his son John's 'meat, drink, clothes and learning as for other students at Oxford'. His estate was to be passed in succession to his wife Margaret, until John was 21 years of age, then to John and the 'heirs of his body' then to daughter Elizabeth and to her heirs and finally, in default of such heirs, 'to the next right heirs of my wife'. I could find no record of John's matriculation in the Alumni Oxoniensis; did he survive to adulthood? If Arthur was right about John Ridoen, was Robert's son the subject of a 1518 confirmation of arms? Unfortunately, the College of Arms has no record of arms granted (or confirmed) to either Robert or John Ridoen; the York Herald did say that the 1494 confirmation was plausible but that the Harleian manuscripts in the British Library should be examined carefully before conclusions could be drawn.

I visited the British Library and saw both Harley mansucripts. In 1116, on the back of folio 38 (not 37d) was a drawing of the griffin arms as previously described although the colours on the arms in trick were labelled 'az' and 'g' i.e. azure (blue) and gules (red). The inscription was "*Robert ~~Roydon~~ Ridoen of the Cytie of Excestre gentleman whosse ancestors were oft inhabyete in the Countie of Devysshe. Azure and gules party per pale a gryff. on counter of the same upon the helm the crest a gryffon likewise in a goldy crown. Given the last day July in AD 1494 the ninth yere of Henery the 7.*" Whilst the year, according to EB Royden, is confirmed, the shield appears to be incorrectly coloured. MSS 5887, on the other hand, showed a pen drawing of the arms, including a gold ducal crown, with the 'usual' shield tinctures of silver and red. The text read "*Robert Rydoen of Exeter given the 9 of H8 by Richmond and (?)Claron. Roydon or Rydon but I find it Roydon.*" So from these documents it is not clear which year is correct, except that, of course, Robert Rydon died well before 1518 and hence 1494 would seem to be appropriate; as the shield colours are usually given as silver and red it appears that there are errors in both mansucripts!

Interestingly, Ernest Bland Royden mentioned in 'Three Royden Families' that this coat of arms is "that which was in the 17th century assigned to the Rydons or Roydons of Battersea and Pyrford, though no connection between the families is known." I wondered if further research on this branch would eventually lead to the Ridouts.

The Roydon or Rydon family of Battersea, in Surrey is the subject of a rags-to-riches story, starting with William; a villein, or feudal tenant who was granted his freedom on the 4th May 1448. John, who may have been William's son, was granted the lease of Battersea manor on 4th October 1499 and was said to be a husbandman whilst his son Henry, a yeoman, held a similar lease from the 7th September 1520. Henry's younger son, also named Henry, was given the lease on the 4th November 1538 after the death of his older brother Robert. By now the estate was growing and in 1563 the younger Henry obtained a twenty-one year lease of all the "tymbre trees and pollardes" growing within the area of Battersea manor; he already held a great deal of the land. When he died in 1568, Henry was described as a gentleman and was the highest tax-payer in Battersea. So, the wealth and social standing of this family progressed, from villein to gentleman in four generations, less than 100 years.

Figure 49: Marble bust of Joan St John

Henry and his wife Elizabeth (neé Knight) had no male heir and so Henry's estate passed to their daughter Joan. She married twice, first to Thomas Holcroft, servant of William Cecil, Lord Burghley, chief advisor of Queen Elizabeth I, and then to Sir Oliver St John (Viscount Grandison and Baron Tregoze). Oliver and Joan were buried together in Battersea in 1630/1 and an entry from 'The Environs of London: vol. 1: County of Surrey' by Daniel Lysons (pub. 1792) states: "*A monument to his memory, is fixed in the north wall of the church, ornamented with busts of himself and his lady (Fig. 49), in white marble; over which are the arms and quarterings of St. John impaling Roydon. The latter were blazoned: Per pale Argent and Sable a griffin segeant, counter-changed*". Elsewhere, the arms of Joan Roydon are described as: Per bend Gules and Argent a Griffin segeant counterchanged [Coll Arms MS 1.8/26b].

ROYDON OF PYRFORD AND CHERTSEY

ARMS.—*Per pale argent and gules, a griffin counter-changed.*

From the Visitation of Surrey in 1623 (*Harl. Soc.* xliii. 179; *Surrey Arch. Collections*, xi.), with additions from Wills, etc.

```
                    Henry Roydon =
                    of Battersea,
                       d. 1531
        ┌──────────────────┴──────────────────┐
    Robert  =  Alice, dau. of ―― Knight    Henry  =  Elizabeth, dau. of ――
  of Battersea,  of Knight's Hill in Surrey  of     Knight, sister of Alice
     d. 1538                               Battersea
            │                                    │
    Elizabeth, = William Roydon            Joan,  = Oliver St. John
    da. and hr.,  of Pyrford,           dau. and hr.  Visct. Grandison
     d. 1612    dead in 1611
```

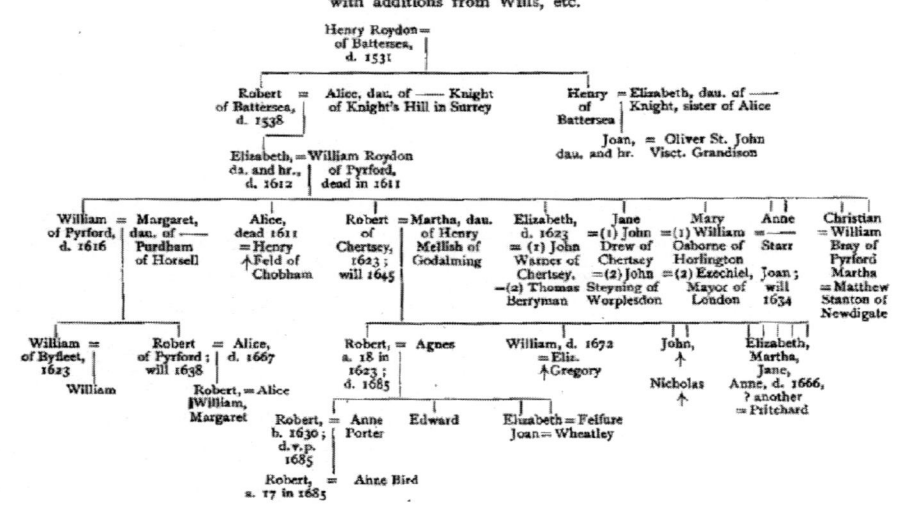

(etc. — descendants of William Roydon of Pyrford and Elizabeth: William of Pyrford d. 1616 = Margaret dau. of ―― Purdham of Horsell; Alice dead 1611 = Henry Feld of Chobham; Robert of Chertsey, 1623; will 1645 = Martha dau. of Henry Mellish of Godalming; Elizabeth d. 1623 = (1) John Warner of Chertsey, = (2) Thomas Berryman; Jane = (1) John Drew of Chertsey, = (2) John Steyning of Worplesdon; Mary = (1) William Osborne of Horlington, = (2) Ezechiel Mayor of London; Anne = ―― Starr, Joan; will 1634; Christian = William Bray of Pyrford = Matthew Stanton of Newdigate.)

Further generations: William of Byfleet 1623 (William); Robert of Pyrford; will 1638 (Robert = Alice [William, Margaret]); Alice d. 1667; Robert a. 18 in 1623; d. 1685 = Agnes (Robert b. 1630 d.v.p. 1685 = Anne Porter; Edward; Robert a. 17 in 1685 = Anne Bird); William d. 1672 = Eliz. Gregory (Elizabeth = Felfure; Joan = Wheatley); John, Nicholas; Elizabeth, Martha, Jane, Anne d. 1666, ? another = Pritchard.

Figure 50: Family tree: Roydon of Battersea, Pyrford & Chertsey

In records of the 1623 visitation of Surrey, the York Herald found a pedigree of four generations headed by William Roydon of Pyrford who married Joan Roydon's cousin, Elizabeth Roydon of Battersea. Arms were recorded as: Per pale Argent and Gules a Griffin segreant counterchanged [Coll Arms MS C2/299b; see also Coll Arms MS Beltz-Pullman Collection C7/114b, now numbered as M.P. VIS 3/114b]. Ernest Bland Roydon constructed a tree showing these families pedigree which is probably similar to that held in the College of Arms (Fig. 50).

So, it seems likely that the griffin arms originated with the Rydon/Roydon family from Devon, who had a collateral branch in Battersea. The York Herald was able to provide further early references to these arms:

- A Manuscript of Arms, dating from the reign of Henry VIII (1509-1547) includes: RYDEN of Exeter in Devon: Per pale Argent and Gules a Griffin rampant and volant (segreant) counterchanged [Coll Arms MS L1/565].
- A large compilation of arms arranged by their design, created by William Flower, Norroy King of Arms (1562-1588) includes: RIDON: Per pale Argent and Gules a Griffin segreant counterchanged [f.51] RIDON: Per pale Argent and Gules a griffin rampant counterchanged. Crest: A demi Griffin de mesme issuant from a Crown Or (dated ~1560) [f. 187v].

Interesting as this research was, it did not indicate a link to the Ridouts of Henstridge. Supposedly, according to Arthur Ridout, Thomas Ridout was a direct descendant of John Ridoen. Of course, it is possible that Thomas could instead have been an unnamed son of Robert Rydon, or another member of this family. Not much is known about Thomas but at least he wrote a will:

"December 20th 1524. Thomas Rydowte of the parishe of Hengystrige within the dioces of bathe. My body to be buried within holy grave. To the cathedral church of Wells 12d. To the high awter of Hengistrige for my tithings forgotten 6s 8d and to every light in the same church 4d. To the bretherhed of our lady in the same church a kowe and to the mayntenyng of the store of St James there a kowe and to the store of St Clement there a kowe. To the store of St Blase at Kyngton a kowe. To the church of Stowre Weston 3s 4d. To John Darke parish clerk of Hengistrige 2s. To every of my god-childern being alive 4d. To my brother Nicolas a kowe, to Elizabeth Payne a kowe, to Joan Mone a bullock and to Kateryn Wolryge a ewe and a lambe. To my eldest sonne my second wayn with all things of apparel therto belonging. To my secunde son John a bullock and six shepe. To my yongest sonne John best wayn with all things of apparel therto belonging and to the same John £3 6s 8d. To my sonne Richard a bullock. To my youngest daughter Johane 66s 8d. The residue of all my goods, chattels and debts not to before bequested my legacies fulfilled my funeral expenses and debts paid I give and bequeath to Isabell my Wife who I ordeyn and make myn whole executrix. She to do for the wealth of my soule as she thinketh best. Witnesses: Sir (?) John Burket curat there, John Wolrige and John Darke. Proved May May 10th 1525."

It is clear that Thomas farmed and was in possession of two 'waynes' (wagons), six cows, three bullocks and eight sheep, including a ewe and a lamb. A modern monetary equivalent of his cash bequests was about £2,500 in 2005, according to the National Archives online currency converter. Thomas had a brother Nicholas and a wife Isabell. Assuming that Richard was not Thomas' oldest son, then the couple had at least four boys and more than one girl (Johane was the youngest daughter). The York Herald confirmed that Thomas was armigerous, and wrote that:

"At the visitation of Somerset, Dorset, Devon and Cornwall undertaken by the heralds in 1531 an entry was recorded for Thomas Ridout of the parish of Henstridge, co. Somerset. He married the daughter of [?] Coope near Woodbery Hill and had issue his son Thomas, who married the daughter of Woolridge. Their three sons are named as William, Thomas and Richard. The arms of Ridout are shown in a sketch as: Per pale Argent and Gules a Griffin segreant counterchanged within a Bordure engrailed Or. No Crest is shown. [Coll Arm Ms H18/52]."

Since the older Thomas died six years before the visitation of the heralds in 1531, presumably the details of the family's pedigree were provided by his eldest son, who we can probably assume was Thomas, although he wasn't named as such in his father's will. Thomas Ridout married Isabell Coope (or Roope; the clerk's hand for 'c' and 'r' are very similar in lower case) and perhaps we can also hazard a guess that the younger Thomas married Katherine Woolridge and that maybe her father or brother was John, who witnessed Thomas' will. By 1531, the younger Thomas' sons William, Thomas and Richard had obviously been born but unfortunately the parish records for Henstridge date from 1605 and so their ages cannot be estimated. Miss Coope was from Woodbury Hill; there is a place of this name near the town of Bere Regis in Dorset, about 23 miles from Henstridge which was the site of an Iron Age hill-fort which seems to have been otherwise uninhabited. Woodbury Hill in the village of Woodbury, on the other hand, is 8 miles SE of Exeter, which may be of relevance. Perhaps Isabell's family were Devonian and indeed there was a noteworthy Roope family in Dartmouth. The question remains: why were the arms of Rydon inherited by a Ridout?

The gold coloured engrailed border on Thomas' arms is an example of how a younger son might 'difference' (modify) the arms of his father in order to distinguish his own line. This implies that Thomas' father, whoever he was, was a member of the Rydon family of Devon, but his identity is unlikely to be proven as no pedigree exists, as far as I know. However, an intriguing link between the families was suggested by Arthur Jewers who listed grants of arms for many families; his work was published serially in The Genealogist journal; in volume 25 (pub. 1909, p. 63) he included the following entry: "RIDOUT, REYDEN or RYDEN alias RYDOUT, of …. co. Somerset. Certif. by Robert Browne Bluemantle[i]. Per pale Arg. and Gu. a griffin segr. counterchanged, within a bord. eng. Or. Crest – A horse's head erased Arg., on the neck an ogress[j]. Stowe MS 677[k]"). I visited the British Library to see the Stowe mansucript for myself; it is a bound book of parchment pages, each showing heraldic shields and crests, beautifully illustrated by different heralds. My rather less artistic rendering of folio 23 is shown in Figure 51. The words in Latin I interpreted as: 'The arms, without (full heraldic) achievement of the family of Ryden alias Rydout of the county of Somerset; 'without achievement' I took to mean that the drawing only depicted the shield, crest and torse without a helmet, mantling or other paraphernalia.

Figure 51: Drawing of Stowe MSS 677 folio 23

Drawn between 1641 and 1646, this may be the earliest existing depiction of the griffin arms as other drawings are undated; the wording clearly shows that at the time the names Ryden (or Royden) were considered to be synonymous with Rydout. Surname spellings were far more flexible and usage was inconsistent in the 17th century, hence the Rydens and Rydouts are likely to have been the same family; 'Ride-on' and 'Ride-out' are, after all, very similar and the horse's head crest may well refer to the supposed origins of the name i.e. a man who rode a horse.

Between my research and that of Arthur Ridout and Peter O'Donoghue, the York Herald, here follows a short list of individuals known to have used these Griffin arms. With the exception of [6] and [7], whose ancestral roots are unknown, these individuals are from the same family and are shown on a tree below the text:

[1] Walter Ridout of Shaftesbury (1606-1680): Release of Dower by Jone Ridout widow of Walter Ridout of Shaston, gent. 30 May 19 James (1621). Jone Ridout in consideration of the sum of 20 marks in hand before delivery of these presents of Thomas Pitt of Blandford & John Cooke of Westminster, Gents. Releases & quit claims etc to Pitt & Cooke & John Ridout son of the above Walter all her rights of Dower etc in Gyles Breke or Whitings containing 7 acres more of less, late in tenure of John Combe, recites the premises in Shaston now in occupation of John Everard. Thomas Barns & one Clark alias Kelwaie - another messuage newly erected by Robert Dole & all other lands in which Pitt & Cooke or John Ridout have any estate freehold or inheritance. She quit claims to all of them to Pitt Cooke & John Ridout who are to have and to hold all of them. Sealed with Ridout Arms: Griffin segreant, no bordure visible. [Records of the Fox-Pitt-Rivers family of Rushmore D/PIT. Dorset History Centre].

[2] Theophilus Ridout (1690-1737): Amongst a collection of family pedigrees, according to the York Herald, is the following: 'A pedigree of four generations headed by Theophilus Ridout of Salisbury Court, Fleet Street, surgeon, whose will was proved in 1737. He had issue by his wife Love including John Ridout of Deptford, co. Kent, who married Mary only child of John Curtis late of Enfield co. Middlesex. The entry descends to the children of their son John Christopher Ridout of Eltham, co. Kent, who died in Sidmouth in 1817, having married Carolina daughter of John Floyd.' [Coll Arm Ms Beltz-Pulman Collection JP87/412].

[3] John Ridout (1703-1773): Witchampton, Dorset. Hutchins History of Dorset Volume III page 479 mentions a monument 'Sacred to the memory of John Ridout Esq of Deans Leaze in this parish. He died on the 30th of January 1773 aged 70 and was buried at Blandford Forum in this county which was the place of his nativity.' 'Sacred also to the memory of Elizabeth his widow who survived him more than eighteen years at whose request this stone was erected; she died November 17th 1791 in the 75th year of her age and is buried under the north window in the body of this Church'. Arms: Ridout impaling Kellaway. Per pale Azure and Sable a Griffin Segreant counterchanged within a bordure engrailed Or Ridout. Argent two crimping irons in Saltire between four pears Gules within a bordure engrailed of the second Kellaway. John's daughter and sole heiress, Elizabeth, married Richard Bingham of Melcombe Bingham, about ten miles west of Blandford. Her arms, showing the (red and white/silver) griffin with gold engrailed border, were displayed on an inescutcheon, or small shield, laid over the complex shield of the Bingham family. The dexter (right) side of the shield represents the quartering of four families: Bingham, Turberville, Pottinger and Chaldecott. The sinister (left) side of the shield are the arms of Halsey. These names indicate previous families that had married into the Binghams, the earliest was the union between Richard de Bingham and Lucy Turberville in about 1246!

Figure 52: Bookplate of Christopher Ridout

[4] Christopher Ridout (1726/7-1790): Lavender Hill, Battersea, London. This image (Fig. 52) was in The Bookplate Journal (1998). The macabre picture shows a medical man, standing half dissected amongst severed heads, bones and cadavers. Christopher was a surgeon in the Borough of Lavender Hill; formerly in the Royal Navy; born on the 10th March 1726/7, son of Theophilus Ridout [2], and

died on the 4th December 1790. He is buried at St Brides Fleet Street. His motto was: Medio tutissimus ibis, meaning 'you will go most safely by the middle way'.

Figure 53: Armorial signet ring

If this shield was drawn according to heraldic convention, the colours depicted, from left to right, would be red (vertical lines) and silver (blank) which would be the wrong way round. It is unlikely that a heraldic illustrator would not have known this but there is another example of such an error. Several years ago, a gold armorial signet ring was found in Bedfordshire (Fig. 53) which dated to the late 16th or early 17th century. The shield is coloured gold (horizontal lines) and silver and the counterchanged griffin silver and gold, but precious metals should not be laid one over the other, according to the Rouge Dragon Pursuivant, so it is likely that the arms were unauthorised.

[5] John Christopher Ridout (~1753-1817): The York Herald reported that a grant of Arms was made by Letters Patent dated 13th August 1783 to John Christopher Ridout of Eltham, co. Kent, eldest son and heir of John Ridout late of Deptford, co. Kent, formerly of London, surgeon, deceased. 'The limitations of the grant were extended to the other descendants of his late father. The Arms are blazoned: Per pale Argent and Gules a Griffin segreant counterchanged on a Chief Vert two Horse's heads couped Argent bridled Or. Crest: on a Wreath of the Colours a Horse's head Argent on the neck two Trefoils slipped proper.' [Coll Arm Ms Grants 15/193].

[6] George Ridout (1658-1729): Plymouth, Devon. Inscription on a tombstone in front of the Communion rails in Charles' Church 'Here lyeth George Ridout attorney-at-law for many years a practitioner in this town age 71, date 1729'. Coat of Arms: per pale Argent and Gules a Griffin counterchanged within a bordure engrailed Or. His son Jonathan who died on the 17th September 1763 was buried in the same vault. This family tree starts with George Ridout who was reputedly born in Sherborne in ~1658, although there is no record of a baptism and his parents are unknown.

[7] Susannah Ridout (1660-1718): In Milton Clevedon church, Somerset is a monument inscribed: 'to the memory of Dame Susannah relict of Thomas Strangways Esq of Melbury in the County of Dorset where they lie interred. She was the best of wives a tender and true indulgent Mother a sincere friend and to this parish a great benefactor. Born November 1660, daughter of John Ridout (John Ridout of Henstridge & Dorsetshire born 1607 died 1670 aged 63) she married Thomas Strangways of Melbury Dorset in 1674. Susannah died on the 19th August 1718 in the 58th year of her age.' A Coat of Arms (described in Collinsons History of Somerset) states 'now (1888) partly obliterated): Sable two Lions passant in pale of six Argent and Gules: Strangways impaling Ridout: Per pale Argent and Gules a Griffin segreant counterchanged within a bordure engrailed Or.'

The man at the head of this tree is Walter, who died ~October 1619; the administration of his estate was passed to widow, Joan or Joanna, of Shaftesbury on the 30th April of that year. Their son Walter was born in 1606; assuming that his father Walter was an adult at the time, he may have been born in 1585 or before; perhaps he was the son, or grandson, of one of the younger Thomas Ridout of Henstridge's sons, William, Thomas or Richard.

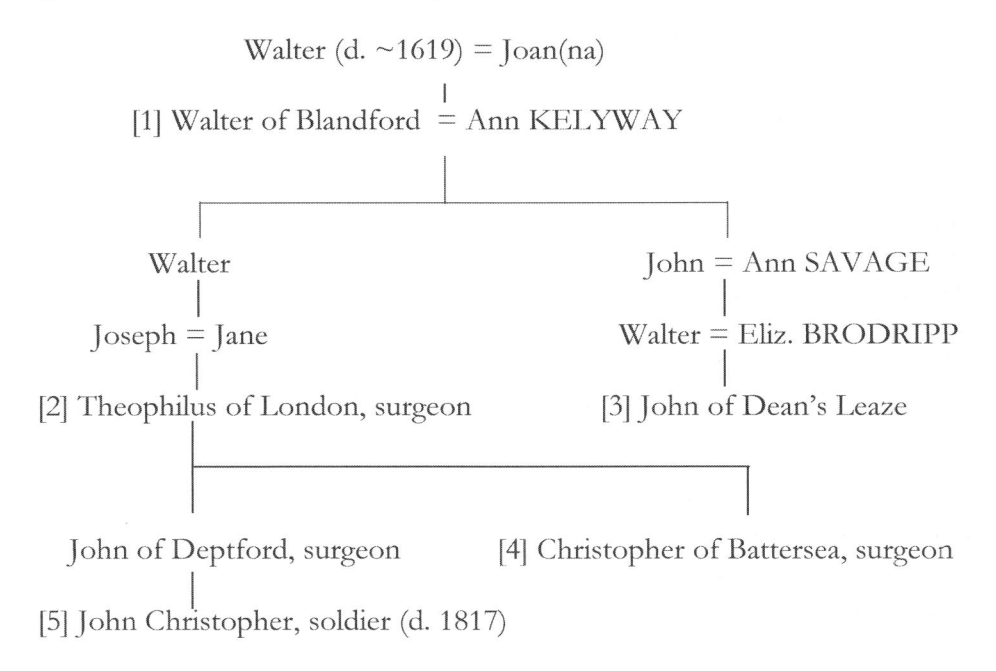

```
                    Walter (d. ~1619) = Joan(na)
                                |
              [1] Walter of Blandford = Ann KELYWAY
                                |
            ┌───────────────────────────────────┐
          Walter                              John = Ann SAVAGE
            |                                   |
        Joseph = Jane                       Walter = Eliz. BRODRIPP
            |                                   |
   [2] Theophilus of London, surgeon    [3] John of Dean's Leaze
            |                                   |
            └───────────────────┬───────────────┘
                                
     John of Deptford, surgeon      [4] Christopher of Battersea, surgeon
            |
   [5] John Christopher, soldier (d. 1817)
```

In conclusion, there seems to be at least a hypothetical line of descent here, from the Rydons of Exeter, to Thomas of Henstridge, to Walter of Shaftesbury and Blandford. However, there is no proof of a link between Walter of Shaftesbury and William Rydowte of Sherborne (1554-1621). Maybe the Sherborne line is instead related to this second group of Ridouts…

Arms: Azure a Trefoil Argent between three Mullets Or

A second coat of arms attributed to the Ridout name, was mentioned only briefly by Arthur Ridout (Ridout book pp. 217, 220). In heraldic texts the blazon often includes a crest, for example in Robson's The British Herald, (1830) is written 'Arms: Azure a Trefoil Argent between three Etoiles Or. Crest: a mount Vert (green) a Horse passant Argent bridled Or.' Similarly, in Burke's General Armory (1884) 'Azure a Trefoil slipped Argent between three Mullets Or. Crest: a Savage's head issuing pp. Or' and: 'Azure a Trefoil Argent between three Etoiles Or. Crest: on a mount Vert a Horse pass. Argent bridled Or'.

Figure 54: Arms of Ridout

Note that the trefoil (shamrock) may be slipped (the end of the stalk is pointed) or not; the three devices around it are mullets (spur rowels) or étoiles (stars). Traditionally, five straight rays indicate a mullet, pierced i.e. with a central hole, or not; six wavy rays usually depicts a star (as in Fig. 54). The Ridout crest varies between a savage (wild man)'s head or a silver coloured trotting horse with a gold bridle (standing on a green mound, or not). Fairburn's Book of the Crests of the Families of Great Britain and Ireland (1892) identifies the trotting horse crest as belonging to a Sussex branch of Rideouts (Fig. 55).

Although it is probably of little value to try and see a significance in these things, it is interesting that three mullets also figured on the arms of George

Figure 55: Trotting horse & savage's head crests, shown on a wreath of the colours

Washington and would become the stars of the American flag. The mullets can represent 'divine quality from above' and the trefoil, some say, indicates 'perpetuity'.

I asked Mr O'Donoghue to research these arms (with or without a crest) as I wanted to know when they had first been used by any man named Rid(e)out. The answer was surprising and, I thought, rather exciting. He wrote "A significant late seventeenth-century manuscript alphabet of Arms in five volumes, known as the EDN Alphabet, includes the following: REDOUT alias RIDEOUT, Dorset: Azure a Trefoil Argent between three Mullets Or. Crest: On a Mount proper a Horse passant Bay colour bridled Or. Of Sherborne. Subscribed by Flower [presumably William Flower, Norroy King of Arms 1562-1588]."

If the York Herald is correct in identifying 'Flower' as William Flower, this means that the arms were in existence, at least, by 1588 and were associated specifically with a Dorset family who lived in Sherborne. I had told Mr O'Donoghue that Walter Ridout of Sherborne (1564-1643; see Chapter 20) had maintained that he had been granted Arms, although unfortunately, he didn't state when this was. On the 24th June 1642, Walter made a written statement (see Chapter 21) in which he wrote:

"…. He that has five plough lands of inheritance may by the Ancient Law write 'gentleman', which I had and more before I passed it to my sons. And the herald came down in the country many years ago and compelled myself and Thomas Swetnam to take arms.

Heretofore I assume no more than is lawful for we were both bred at the university and at the Inns of Court...."

Walter matriculated Brasenose College on 18th July 1580 and went on to the Inns of Court, returning to Sherborne in Dorset to work as an attorney. In 1603 he inherited a good deal of land and property from his tenant-in-chief uncle William Rydowte of Chettle and Sherborne. Walter was right to say that he was classed as a gentleman by virtue of his wealth, property and University education; this means that he was armigerous i.e. entitled to bear Arms. The Herald continues...

"We can draw certain conclusions. The first relates to the Arms: Azure a Trefoil (slipped) Argent between three Mullets. These Arms appear in published sources first, it would seem, in Edmondson 1780 (Joseph Edmondson); prior to that the Arms and Crest appear in the late seventeenth-century EDN Alphabet. Despite this, no entry has been found for the Arms or Crest in the official records of the College of Arms. Searches of our records of Arms and Crests arranged by their designs also failed to reveal anything for this. This might be because a) the Arms are not genuine, having been adopted or made up either by heraldic painters or by a family, without ever having them granted or confirmed; or because b) the Arms were at some time properly granted but the record of them has not survived. Records of pre-1670s grants of Arms are not absolutely 100% complete. The entry mentions Sherborne, Dorset; and this might suggest that the Arms there for Redout or Ridout were in fact used by the Walter Ridout or Sherborne that you mention in your document. A close examination of the Dorset visitation records revealed no reference to Ridout or indeed to Thomas Swetnam, who is there referred to."

I think it unlikely that Walter Ridout had lied about this matter; indeed he had no need to be dishonest. Although it is possible that these arms were not formerly granted, or recorded at the College, clearly they could still be those that were adopted by Walter. I decided to search for any individual that may have used these arms in more recent times and I found references to four men from Arthur Ridout's notes, from Mr O'Donoghue's research and elsewhere.

[1] Richard Ridout (1715-1767): Apparently, his bookplate was sent to Arthur Ridout by General Arthur Kennedy Rideout R.A. April 1895 (see [3] in the tree below), Arms: Rideout quartering Rochester (Fig. 56). Richard was the son of Richard Ridout (1698-1753) and Anne Acton (neé Rochester). Father and son were Barons of the Cinque Port and attended their sovereigns during the coronations respectively of George I (1714) George II (1727). In 'The History and Antiquities of the Town and Port of Hastings Illustrated by a

Series of Engravings, from Original Drawings' (Moss, 1824) also states that a Ridout (no first name) was a Baron of the Port of Hastings and canopy bearer for the queen at the coronations of King George III and Queen Charlotte in 1761. The bookplate in Figure 56 shows an exact 19th century reproduction of the original Jacobean engraving; the bookplate itself probably belonged to Henry Wood Rideout, an officer in the 19th Dragoons and son of [2]. Note the use of a motto: Toutz Foitz Chevalier (Always a Knight) and three mullets.

Figure 56: Arms of Henry Wood Rideout

This bookplate (Fig. 57) shows the arms of Ridout impaling Nicholl but the identity of the bookplate owner is unknown. Here there are three étoiles, rather than mullets!

[2] Richard Rideout (1759-]: married Sarah, widow of Samuel Nicoll and daughter of Francis Carter Nicoll.

[3] Rev'd John Rideout (1768-1838): Nephew of Richard [1], he was the rector, then curate, of Woodmancote Church in Horsham, West Sussex between 1793 and 1815. He matriculated Jesus College Cambridge and gained a BA (1790) and a MA (1795). He married a second time to a widow Frances Dring (daughter of Sir Harry Goring Bart.). Arms: Azure between three mullets or a trefoil argent for Rideout impaling Argent a chevron between three annulets for Goring.

Figure 57: Arms of Richard Ridout

ARTHUR KENNEDY RIDEOUT, *Esquire, Major-Gen., on the retired list, late of the Royal Artillery, Knight of the Legion of Honour, has medals for the Crimea (with clasps for Inkerman and Sebastopol) and Indian Mutiny, also Turkish Medal for Crimea. Born April 18, 1835, being the fourth son of the late Henry Wood Rideout, late of 19th Regt. and of Chestham Park, Sussex, and Lansdown, Bath, by his wife Frances Letitia, only child of late Capt. Waring of the 24th Light Dragoons. Clubs—United Service, Junior United Service, Army and Navy, Cavalry, and Garrick. Livery—Dark blue coat, red waistcoat, gilt buttons, and black trousers; overcoat dark blue.* **Armorial bearings** *as used, but for which no authority has as yet been officially established, are for* **Arms**—*A trefoil slipped proper, between three mullets or.* **Crest**—*On a mount vert, a horse passant proper, bridled gules.* **Motto**—"*Toutz foitz chevalier.*" *Married, April 8, 1875, Mary Ellen, widow of W. S. Jackson of Moor House, Headingley, Leeds; and has* Issue—*Ernest Henry Rideout, Sub-Lieut. Royal Navy, b. Feb. 8,*

Figure 58: Arms of Arthur Kennedy Rideout

[4] Arthur Kennedy Rideout (1835-1913): Son of Henry Wood Rideout of Bath and Frances Letitia Waring, Henry was a soldier of great distinction and appeared in the book 'Armorial Families: a Directory of Some Gentlemen of Coat-Armour' written by Arthur Charles Fox-Davies (Edinburgh, 1899). This entry not only gives Arthur's biography and military achievements but also describes and illustrates the coat of arms which he used with the warning: "Armorial bearings as used, but for which no authority has as yet been offically established…" (Fig. 58).

[5] Frank Montrésor Rideout (b. 1885): the York Herald wrote that a grant of arms was made to Frank Montrésor Montrésor (formerly Rideout), by Letters Patent dated 15 March 1916. [Coll Arm Ms Grants 84/126]. Frank was also a soldier of distinction who won the MC in WW2; he was a nephew of Arthur Kennedy Rideout and son of Maj. Gen. Francis Goring Rideout and his wife Emily.

With a few exceptions, these men seems to be either heir to their father's estate with no particular occupation, a military officer or a churchman; this sounds like the sort of pattern that one might expect of landed gentry of this time. The relationships to each other and to Walter Rydowte of Sherborne and Folke are shown by this tree:

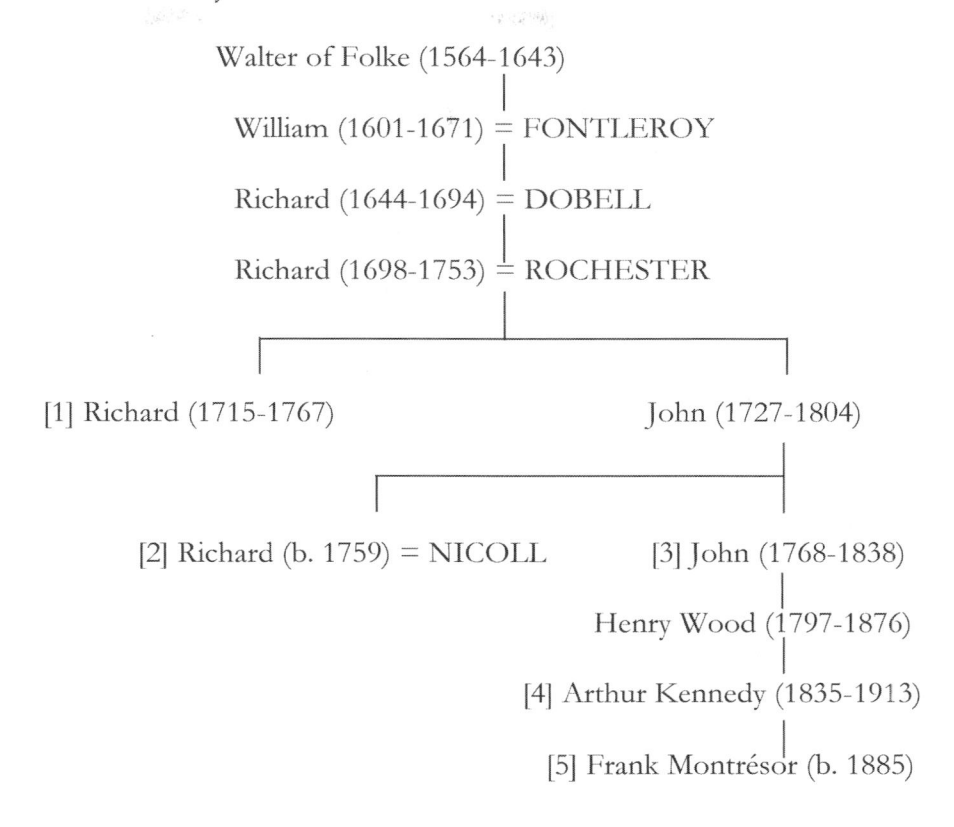

```
                    Walter of Folke (1564-1643)
                                |
                    William (1601-1671) = FONTLEROY
                                |
                    Richard (1644-1694) = DOBELL
                                |
                    Richard (1698-1753) = ROCHESTER
                                |
              ┌─────────────────┴─────────────────┐
     [1] Richard (1715-1767)              John (1727-1804)
                                                  |
                                    ┌─────────────┴─────────────┐
                    [2] Richard (b. 1759) = NICOLL      [3] John (1768-1838)
                                                                |
                                                      Henry Wood (1797-1876)
                                                                |
                                                    [4] Arthur Kennedy (1835-1913)
                                                                |
                                                     [5] Frank Montrésor (b. 1885)
```

Research suggested a tenuous connection between William of Chettle, Walter Rydowte's uncle, and my ancestor William of Hyle (1554-1621; see Chapter 19) yet I could find no evidence that they were actually blood relations, however much I believed this to be true. William of Chettle was a man of means, a tenant-in-chief and therefore, as his will indicates, a gentleman. Until very recently, I had no idea about the social standing of my ancestor; when William of Hyle wrote his will he described himself simply as a yeoman and whilst this may have been a cut above a husbandman socially, nevertheless William was a working man and therefore not considered armigerous. However, I have found some references in the book 'Sherborne Almshouse Register' edited by Ann Clark (Dorset Record Society, 2013) that are very thought provoking.

On the 19th April 1613 a resolution was made between the brethren of the Sherborne Almshouse to levy fines for those who refused to take on the duty of Master, if required to do so; one of the brothers named was William Rydowte. In 1613 William of Chettle had been dead for a decade and his nephew's son William was only 12 years of age so who was this man? Other entries, detailing the Almshouse business, under the same name in December 1610 and October 1612. The Almshouse maintained a list of those men who were selected to serve as brethren, the date appointed and the date left (usually when the brother had died). On the 19th December 1603, Richard Couth was chosen in place of William Rydowte, 'late a brother and deceased' (William of Chettle was buried five days before this and so this entry no doubt relates to him). On the 9th February 1606, 'William Rydowte was chosen a brother into the house in place of John Thorne, deceased.' William was in turn replaced by Robert Hoddinott on the 10th July 1621 (William of Hyle and Sherborne was buried on the 30th June). So, it seems likely that William of Sherborne, my ancestor, was an Almshouse brother for fifteen years. This is significant because only leading citizens of the town carried this responsibility; William would also have been a governor of Sherborne School since the two roles went hand in hand. From the late 17th century, such upstanding citizens would probably have been afforded the title of 'Esquire'; so perhaps William wasn't so humble after all!

Another interesting observation is that William of Chettle's nephew, Walter was chosen to serve as a brother in the almshouse on the 7th December 1605 and was made Master on the 4th July 1608 (according to historian C H Mayo MA D.Litt. who compiled a list of masters). William Rydowte of Sherborne was chosen to serve as a brother only two months after Walter's entry; I wonder if Walter was in any way influential in bringing William into the house? I can not prove that William and Walter were related, nor can I prove 'beyond all reasonable doubt' that the Henstridge/Blandford and Sherborne Ridouts were not one and the same family but perhaps us folk who descend from William of Sherborne might like to at least consider riding under the banner of the trefoil and mullets instead of the griffin.

Footnotes:

h. The Harley Manuscripts are papers collected by Robert Harley (1661-1724) from about 1704, augmented by later generations and stored at the British Library in London.

i. Robert Browne held the post of Bluemantle Pursuivant between 1641 and 1646 and hence the drawing must have been made between those dates.

j. An ogress is not a female giant in this context but a pellet or gunstone

k. The same reference used by Arthur Ridout re: Thomas Ridout of Henstridge's pedigree. His exact entry is as follows [Ridout book, p. 219]: 'In Stowe M.S. 677 f 27 County Somerset 14 June Charles II (1662): Visitation by Robert Browne Blewmantle. A sketch of arms 'Per pale Argent & Gules a Griffin segreant counterchanged within a bordure engrailed Or. Crest a Horse's head couped Argent. Royden in left corner als Rydout on right.'

22. Summary and Conclusions

This book is a record of my research into my maternal grandfather's Ridout family; a second volume, in preparation, will relate to our 'later' history i.e. from ~1800 when my x3 great grandfather John moved from Sherborne to Bath.

The first three chapters introduced John and his brothers Charles and Samuel and established that our branch is connected with a large Sherborne dynasty which has many members in the United States of America and Canada and, of course, in Great Britain. DNA testing has indicated that our branch diverged from the rest, with 90% probability, between about 1654 and 1714, possibly more recently.

Chapter four related to our most distant known, common ancestor William (1554-1620) a yeoman who lived in Sherborne and may have farmed a small area of land in an estate around Hyle Farm. William was married to Agneta Barnard, who died two years before him and was buried in Sherborne Abbey. In his will, William mentioned their two sons Thomas (b. 1574) and William (b. 1577) plus numerous grandchildren. The next three chapters recorded the history of William's probably best known descendant, Christopher (1669-1743) a miller and baker. In Chapter five, a popular misunderstanding about Christopher was shown to be untrue: that he was from Henstridge in nearby Somerset and was baptised there in 1664, son of Christopher and Edith (or Judith) Blackmore. Rather Christopher was a son of John, a husbandman, and his wife Elizabeth and was baptised in Sherborne Abbey in 1699; he married twice first to Mary Parsons (m.1694) and then to Mary Glover (m.1697). Apart from son George (b.1701) Christopher and Mary had a daughter Elizabeth (b.1705) and a son John (b. 1699). John may have been the first American settler in our family, although sadly his history is largely unrecorded.

Christopher, George and his son George lived and worked in what was then known as Ridout's Mill (later renamed West Mill); which sits in dilapidated state, but with waterwheel intact, on the River Yeo, south of the town. Despite being a yeoman – a man of some substance – Christopher died in the workhouse. The link between Christopher and his ancestor William of Hyle was discussed in Chapter eight. It seems likely that Christopher descended from William's son Thomas, although from which of Thomas's many sons is uncertain – either Thomas (b. 1601) and his wife Eleanor, or William (b. 1599) and his wife Julyan. In Chapter nine, more of George the baker's history was outlined and some details of his estate, including the Mill were given.

In Chapter ten a second Ridout myth was debunked: John Ridout (b. 1730) son of George the baker was not a Huguenot, as some texts have suggested. A popular story is that our ancestors were French non-conformists who fled their homeland to settle in Sherborne when the Edict of Nantes (which offered religious freedom to Protestants) was revoked by King Louis XIV in 1685. Clearly, our Ridout family occupied a place in Sherborne well before then, at least as far back as the mid sixteenth century and probably much earlier. This misunderstanding probably came about by the misreading of the word 'Fontmealle' (as in Fontmell Magna) as 'Fontainebleu' in the 1582 will of Walter Ridout of Langham, Gillingham. It is true that there are Ridoutt and Ridoux families to whom this history might pertain but they are not related to us and are not discussed further.

Chapters eleven to thirteen dealt with my own Ridout family line. My x3 great grandfather John was baptised in 1785 to John and Susanna Ridout in Sherborne. The Sherborne parish records list the ages at death for two men named John (bur. 1827, aged 73 or bur. 1826, aged 76, suggesting a birth year of either 1754 or 1751) and one woman, Susanna (bur. 1817 suggesting a birth year of ~1753); this provided a starting point for research into John Ridout, my x4 great grandfather and for two (very) hypothetical lines back to Wiliam of Hyle. My research pointed toward a family in Nethercombe, a hamlet north of Sherborne, and the identification of John Ridout (1657-1709) and his wife Elizabeth (née Porter) as my likely ancestors. Wills and Sherborne estate records identified John's parents as John (bur. 1672) and Alice (née Toogood) of Nethercombe.

The older John was a husbandman; he and his brother Thomas (bur. 1668) helpfully left wills; these documents were important in constructing a family tree which was expanded further in Chapter 14 with the discovery of a London branch of Ridouts descending from John and Elizabeth's son Porter (b. 1699/00) whose own son Porter (b. 1733) lived in the parish of Duke's Place in Aldgate and was the keeper of a coffee house; a very interesting murder case centred on Porter causing him to leave the area before his death in 1793. His son Jeremiah (1762-1842) was described as an 'American merchant', presumably meaning that he dealt with the import and export trade. Initially Jeremiah lived in the same area as his father but eventually moved to Birmingham with his wife and daughters where he stayed until his death.

As well as Porter, John and Elizabeth had a son John (b. 1691); I had already speculated that he could be my x6 great grandfather in Chapter 12 but at that time I didn't know the identity of John and Elizabeth. Now I had an additional candidate; Porter Ridout of Sherborne, as well as having a son Porter in 1733, also had a son John who was baptised in 1731 – could this be my x5 great grandfather? He was a blacksmith by trade, undertaking an apprenticeship in Sherborne with Matthew King in 1746; John is also mentioned in his cousin Jeremiah's will in 1786. A tree summarising what I believe is my family can be found on the last page of this book.

By a strange coincidence I found another member of this line living in London: Thomas (1667-1734), son of John and Alice, became a maker of fine shoes, some of which are still displayed in the New York Metropolitan Museum. Thomas also had a son named Jeremiah (1695-1788) who was a woollen draper working and living in Cloth Fair, near Great St Bartholomew's Church, Farringdon.

Chapter fifteen dealt with the correct placing on the larger family tree of John Ridout, husband of Elizabeth ?Oliver (Sherborne line) and John Ridout, husband of Alice Toogood (Nethercombe line). To illuminate this research, in Chapter sixteen, the Oliver family of Sherborne was expanded and marriages into the Ridout family were followed down to James Ridout (1765-1836) a draper of Sherborne; his North Wootton family was then traced back up to an earlier point in Chapter seventeen. In Chapter eighteen I took the North Wootton line even further back, to the early seventeenth century, and attempted to untangle two Richard Ridouts, one a grandson of William Ridout of Hyle. Whilst the North Wotton line does occasionally cross paths with the Sherborne family, I could not prove a familial link between them, even though I believe that one might exist.

Chapters nineteen and twenty introduced two new men: William Rydowte of Chettle (~1553-1603) and his nephew Walter (1564-1643), both of whom are surprisingly well documented given the era in which they lived. William was a tenant-in-chief (sometimes call a baron) holding a lot of land from the Crown; he was subject of an Inquisition Post Mortem in 1613. Walter was a very colourful character, an outspoken attorney and rather a rebel; both men were involved with the governance of Sherborne Almshouse and of the newly re-opened School, following the Dissolution of the Monasteries during the reign of King Henry VIII. A plausible link between William and my ancestor, William of Hyle is examined.

The final chapter was written after several months of research into armoury. Two family lines were identified by the coats of arms that they used; one by descendants of Walter Rydowte, as above, and the other by a Rideout line established in Blandford Forum. There is, and has for some time, been a strong belief by some descendants of our Sherborne family that we can be traced back to Henstridge. The earliest known armigerous (arms bearing) Ridout was Thomas of Henstridge; because some people wrongly believed that Christopher the miller was from that town they also assumed that he was a descendant of Thomas. My research and that of the York Herald at the College of Arms in London shows that Thomas was part of a R(o)ydon family from Devon. Descendancy, according to the use of arms, seems to have passed to a Rideout line in Blandford Forum, not the Ridout line in Sherborne. My feeling is that our Sherborne line is connected with William Rydowte of Chettle but this may never be proven.

If substantial new data come to light, a revised edition of this book may be published but, in the mean time, whilst I hope that you have found something interesting here, please keep in mind that this is just my personal research and as such is as subject to mistakes as anyone else's work.

Karen

Dr Karen Francis, November 2014

WILLIAM = AGNETA BARNARD
b.1554

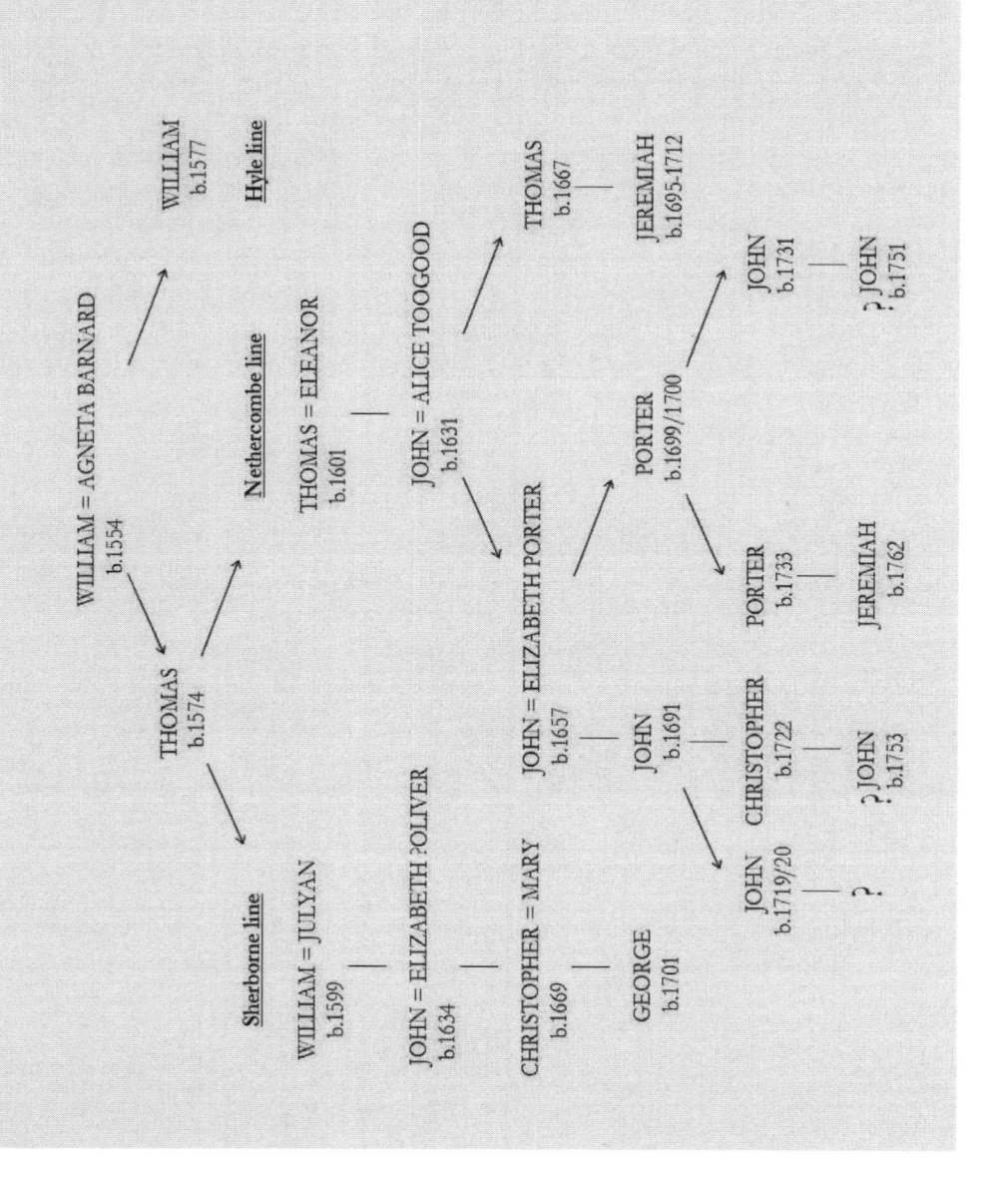

→ WILLIAM b.1577 **Hyle line**

THOMAS b.1574

Nethercombe line

THOMAS = ELEANOR
b.1601

JOHN = ALICE TOOGOOD
b.1631

→ THOMAS b.1667

JOHN = ELIZABETH PORTER
b.1657

JOHN b.1691

→ PORTER b.1699/1700
   JEREMIAH b.1695-1712
   JOHN b.1731
   ? JOHN b.1751

→ PORTER b.1733
   JEREMIAH b.1762

Sherborne line

WILLIAM = JULYAN
b.1599

JOHN = ELIZABETH ?OLIVER
b.1634

CHRISTOPHER = MARY
b.1669

GEORGE b.1701

JOHN b.1719/20   CHRISTOPHER b.1722
?   ? JOHN b.1753

Regal House School
Charlotte St.

(small school)

Good for Moon
Kingsmead St. (